MYTH OF THE WEST

Introduction   Chris Bruce

Essays   Chris Bruce

                                                Brian W. Dippie

                                                Paul Fees

                                                Mark Klett

                                                Kathleen Murphy

RIZZOLI
NEW YORK

The Henry Art Gallery   University of Washington
                                                Seattle

Published in conjunction with the exhibition, *Myth of the West,* held at the Henry Art Gallery, University of Washington, Seattle, September 16-December 2, 1990.

First published in the United States of America in 1990 by Rizzoli International Publications, Inc., 300 Park Avenue South, New York, NY 10010, in conjunction with the exhibition *Myth of the West.*

Major support for *Myth of the West* has come from Pacific First Federal Savings Bank, Seattle. Additional support has come from PONCHO, the Kreielsheimer Foundation, the Foster Foundation, and Gull Industries.

Library of Congress Cataloging-in-Publication Data

Myth of the West/introduction by Chris Bruce; essays by Chris Bruce…[et al.].

    Published in conjunction with the exhibition held at the Henry Art Gallery, Seattle, Sept. 16-Dec. 2, 1990.
    ISBN 0-8478-1259-6.—ISBN 0-8478-1260-X (pbk.)
    1. West (U.S.) in art—Exhibitions. 2. Indians of North America—Pictorial works—Exhibitions. 3. Arts, American—Exhibitions.
    1. Bruce, Chris. II. Henry Art Gallery.
    NX653.W47M98 1990
    700—dc20   90-4343 CIP

Curator: Chris Bruce
Photographic Consultant: Mark Klett
Publication Coordinator: Tamara Moats
Editor: Deborah Easter
Graphic Designer: Douglas Wadden

Cover illustrations
Albert Bierstadt. *Merced River, Yosemite Valley,* 1886 (detail). See page 60.

Andy Warhol. *Double Elvis,* 1963 (detail). See page 174 and 175.

Back cover illustration
Georgia O'Keeffe. *Black Cross with Red Sky,* 1929. See page 8.

Title page illustration
Paul Caponigro. *Monument Valley, Utah,* 1970 (detail). See page 105.

Text set in Century Text and ITC Franklin Gothic with Gill Cameo display
Typography by Thomas & Kennedy Typography, Seattle
Printed by Toppan Printing, Inc., Tokyo, Japan on 100 lb. U-Lite Matte

Foreword

Those of us who grew up in the 1950s, particularly in the western United States, were enraptured and encircled by the myth of the West. Enraptured by the black-and-white images of the Lone Ranger, Hopalong Cassidy, and Davy Crockett, as well as encircled by cowboy wallpaper, toy guns, and Wild West accouterments. In some respect, the 1950s might mark the high watermark of America's unquestioning acceptance of the "opening up" of the West. Since then, more intensive scrutiny has brought greater dimension and historical accuracy to the one-dimensional image of the western hero.

Broadcast and printed, the image of the hero with white hat pervaded countless childhoods, and captivated a young audience, usually boys, who both desired the active role of the cowboy hero, with its loud noises and games of pursuit, and the simplified world view of good guy versus bad guy and cowboy versus Indian. It was a play palette of black-and-white morality, no shades of gray and no self-doubt. It was not the job of children to divine fact in fantasy, but few elders questioned the historical accuracy or cultural bias of the western hero. In fact, they often fueled it by dispensing toy guns and suburbanite western folklore to youthful adventurers.

The ebb in the flood tide of the popularization of the myth of the West began in the 1960s when a national crisis of political purpose and social responsibility unfolded in the struggle for racial equality and the increasing doubts that any nation could serve as global sheriff. In the succeeding decades a more complete picture of the West, its history, heroes, and landscape has emerged. It is a picture of multiple, not single perspectives: an image of loss, as well as gain. In hindsight we see cultural dislocation and environmental ravage, as well as the more familiar histories of exploration, individual valor, and visions of an extraordinary landscape.

Paintings and sketches from the mid-1800s were immensely persuasive visual evidence of a dramatic new frontier to an urban East Coast population. Later, the 19th century's new technologies of photography and film accelerated the popularization of the myth, and as the industrial revolution was overtaken by the electronic revolution, the image, more than the word, took precedence in the popular press.

Multiple generations of artists: explorer-illustrators and photographers, romantic narrative painters, and cinematic pioneers divined, refined, canonized, and replicated the singular images that we came to know so well: the cowboy as the resolute and taciturn "righter of wrongs"; the desperado (a Spanish word of appropriately spiritual implication) as the irredeemable evil-doer; the landscape of inexhaustible beauty and resource—green grass and infinite vista, or conversely an arid hell with bleached bones as landmarks and circling vultures as harbingers of death.

The myth of the West is a history largely written by the victors, and, if the injustices cannot be undone, then the history as written, or drawn, must be reexamined. This exhibition and book consider the role of artists in creating, clarifying, and popularizing the images and symbols of the western saga for a colonial and European audience. Many of these artists came west with 19th-century explorers in search of new and exotic subjects. Others were, or became, what they observed: adventurers in a world of beauty and danger. In the next century, when the fleeting world of the explorer had long vanished, new generations of artists entered the realm of fiction and fantasy to create a mythic world founded on the layers of images and condensed story lines created by their predecessors.

This project was conceived by Senior Curator Chris Bruce and is the result of over three years of research, discussion, and travel. The exhibition's success is due in no small part to his vision and tireless determination to find precisely the right works of art and conceptual framework to illuminate a complex subject. All of us at the Henry Art Gallery are grateful to have had the opportunity to work with Chris on this project.

In the preparation of *Myth of the West*, exhibition and book, we have enjoyed generous support from many individuals representing public and private collections who expressed enthusiasm for the project and a willingness to lend important works of art. For their advice and encouragement we extend our heartfelt thanks to Sara Boehme and Peter Hassrick, Buffalo Bill Historical Center; Rick Stewart, Amon Carter Museum; Anne Morand and Fred Myers, Gilcrease Institute; William Truettner, National Museum of American Art; William Johnson, Walters Art Gallery; David Hunt, Joslyn Art Museum; and William Foxley, Museum of Western Art. All these people are among the leaders in the field of art of the American West and all committed to the project earlier in the planning stages. Without their support, the high quality of loans would have been impossible.

In addition, we would like to thank each lender and artist; Mark Klett, for giving of his time and expertise in advising us on photographic works; and Kathleen Murphy and Richard Jameson, for their assistance in conceptualizing the role of film.

I would especially like to thank all members of the Henry Art Gallery staff for their enthusiastic support of this important exhibition. Assistant Director Joan Caine was both a diligent manager and persistent fundraiser, and was efficiently assisted in the tracking of finances by Carol Strum and Paige Wheeler. Nancy Duncan performed miracles in the preparation and supervision of the correspondence and other tasks for the project. Claudia Bach, assisted by Mary Lloyd, made certain that information about the exhibition reached both press and public. The exhibition logistics were managed flawlessly by Anne Gendreau, and the installation was accomplished by the skill and refinement that is the hallmark of the installation crew headed by Jim Rittiman.

This publication was the result of a large-scale effort, and we were very pleased to be able to work with Gianfranco Monacelli, Solveig Williams, and Lois Brown of Rizzoli International. Chris Bruce provided the conceptual structure for the book in addition to his written contributions. We are indebted to Mark Klett, Kathleen Murphy, Paul Fees, and Brian Dippie for their support of the project and their excellent essays for this book. Tamara Moats tirelessly oversaw the myriad of details relating to the editorial and photographic process. Doug Wadden created a superb design for the book, living up to the challenge of creating both a beautiful and practical form for ideas and images. Deborah Easter was an excellent editor and provided valuable insight as she worked with Chris, Tamara, and the authors to refine the essays. Jennifer Reidel worked ceaselessly, providing careful editorial assistance. Also, we are indebted to Cory Pike for her research assistance and to Sigrid Asmus for the excellent index.

One of the unique aspects of the Henry Art Gallery is the support that is provided by the Henry Gallery Association. We are fortunate to have a Board of Trustees who believe in attaining the highest level of excellence at the Henry Art Gallery. Led by Board President Walter Parsons and Director Phoebe Caner, their hard work and generosity provide the core of support for exhibitions and publications. We are also grateful for the support provided by the University of Washington and are particularly pleased to enjoy the benefit provided by the leadership of Dean Joe Norman and Associate Dean for Arts Arthur Grossman of the College of Arts and Sciences.

Finally, we are most grateful to the public and private organizations that provided financial support for this undertaking. In particular we wish to thank Pacific First Federal Savings Bank for their major support of this exhibition, as well as PONCHO for providing a significant grant for this book; Charles Osborne and the Kreielsheimer Foundation for their longstanding support of the Gallery and this project; Michael Foster and the Foster Foundation; and William L. True and Gull Industries, Inc.

Richard Andrews
Director
Henry Art Gallery

American Geographical Society Collection, University of Wisconsin-Milwaukee Library

American Heritage Center, University of Wyoming

Amon Carter Museum

Archer M. Huntington Art Gallery, The University of Texas at Austin

Buffalo Bill Historical Center

Paul Caponigro

Center for Creative Photography

Colorado State Historical Society

Douglas S. Cramer

Denver Public Library

Etherton Gallery

Fine Arts Museums of San Francisco

The Thomas Gilcrease Institute of American History and Art

Frank Gohlke

Harvard University Art Museums

Henry Art Gallery

Annette Insdorf

Joslyn Art Museum

Gus Kayafas

Mark Klett

The Manoogian Collection

Metropolitan Museum of Art

Laurence Miller Gallery

Richard Misrach

R. Joseph and Elaine R. Monsen

Montana Historical Society

Montana Stockgrowers Association

Museum of Fine Arts, Houston

Museum of Modern Art

Museum of Western Art

National Cowboy Hall of Fame

National Museum of American Art

New York Public Library

The Oakland Museum

Pace/MacGill Gallery

Mr. and Mrs. Gerald Peters

Phoenix Art Museum

Eliot Porter

Private Collection

C. David Robinson

San Antonio Museum of Art

Scheinbaum and Russek

Julie Schimmel

Seattle Art Museum

The University Gallery, University of Delaware

University of Washington Libraries

U.S. Department of the Interior, Geological Survey

U.S. Department of the Interior, National Park Service, Yellowstone National Park

The Walters Art Gallery

Georgia O'Keeffe
Black Cross with Red Sky. **1929**
Oil on canvas
40 x 32 in
Mr. and Mrs. Gerald P. Peters, Santa Fe, New Mexico.

Table of Contents

Albert Bierstadt. *Passing Storm Over the Sierra Nevadas,*
1870 (detail). See page 67.

The Myth of the West

"We never escape the dramatic atmosphere of
our own initiation."[1]
David Thomson, 1987

The notes for the text begin on page 185.

A • preceding an artwork caption indicates that the work was
not included in the exhibition.

Custer Battlefield is a short turn off I-90 in the
Crow Indian reservation, about sixty miles north of
Sheridan, Wyoming, and about sixty miles southeast
of Billings, Montana, or "the middle of nowhere" as a
city dweller is inclined to say about any uninhabited
place not on a large river, lake, or ocean. Sheridan is,
by the way, the general setting for Jack Schaefer's
novel *Shane,* although it hardly looks the part today.
If it weren't for the visitor center and veteran's ceme-
tery, the battlefield environment would seem pretty
well untouched over the last hundred years, located
in a beautiful landscape of rolling grasslands, overlooking the string of trees that line the Little Bighorn
River. Hilly, open fields are scattered with 258 white
gravestones and a single black one, all placed
exactly where members of the Seventh Cavalry and
Custer fell, June 25, 1876. The Sioux removed their
dead immediately.

The day we were there a hot, gentle breeze ruffled
the dry grass and seemed to blanket any sounds that
didn't come from rattlesnakes or small darting birds.
My memory of that day is a sort of haunting bulge
in time that had little to do with the battle; I knew
almost nothing about it. In fact, the emerging sense
of place had more to do with the great gaps in my
knowledge, which meshed perfectly with the vacant
setting itself. I certainly did not consider Custer to be
the hero he was thought to be for almost a century
following his death. If anything, I had accepted history's more recent revision, which casts him as closer
to being an egotistical killer, obsessed with power.
(Now I think he is neither.)

So I was astonished to become aware of how
absolutely moved I was, an experience of landscape
that had only a few precedents for me. Why was this
place so peculiarly awesome? One fact that does not
fully explain the question, is that I had seen many
images of what had happened there, but had never
seen a picture of the place itself, of the void of the
land. Most western landscapes are represented as
monumental or as arenas of intense action, not as
the great vacuum of content which this seemed to
be. It occurs to me now that absence is one of the
great gifts of western landscape, thus allowing
information delivered in bulk loads of paperbacks,

photographs, paintings, films, and TV shows to fill
these wide open spaces with some fact, and lots of
drama, in a continual attempt to explain ourselves
to ourselves.

This ability of the West to create itself in myth
and legend had surely gone on for centuries before
the first artists of the European tradition began to
explore the American West in the 1830s. Yet these
earlier, native myths were based on fundamental kin-
ships with nature, rather than the European push-pull
of conflicting forces: an intrinsic relationship with
place rather than a romantic horizon of endless
opportunities. In this sense our exhibition and publication, which cover artwork from 1832 to the present,
do little more than pick a highly charged pocket of
time (a sort of "evocative 1820s to 1890s") and hold
a mirror to the overriding preconceptions that have
retained visibility to the mainstream culture today.
To understand the American character, one properly
begins here.

Oddly enough, the Henry Art Gallery's exhibition,
Myth of the West, is the first survey of art of the
American West ever presented in Seattle, Washington. Clearly, the West Coast is not *the* West, and this
says a lot about who our primary personage is *not*
(logger, fisherman, sailor). We will ultimately focus
on the figure of the western hero in seeking to identify the myth in work as diverse as that of Alfred
Jacob Miller, Charles Russell, and Andy Warhol. In so
doing we can hardly help but ask what makes this
lone individual so special, why this person—who is
essentially a drifter, a common wage earner at best,
whose greatest gestures of freedom are to take off
his badge, quit the cattle drive, draw his gun, or ride
off into the sunset—is so worthy of our admiration?

Here we come face to face with the two organizing
principles of our project: the transcendental landscape and the composite western hero. You can
hardly have one without the other. The landscape is
the stage set upon which the drama of the western
myth is played out, and it is an essential ingredient
of our story. If there is a sense of destiny in American
affairs, it is because the western hero had the most
vast and majestic backdrop ever imagined, both in
reality and even more in the created images of 19th-
century artists such as Albert Bierstadt and Thomas
Moran, Karl Bodmer and George Catlin. Without the
land, the Westerner would have had about as much

Timothy O'Sullivan
Ancient Ruins of the Cãnon de Chelly,
New Mexico in a Niche 50 Feet Above
Present Canyon Bed. **1876**
Albumen print
7⅞ x 10¾ in
Denver Public Library, Western History Department.

appeal as his contemporaries in West Virginia coal mines or New England textile mills. That is, almost none. Shane wouldn't have fared as well in present-day Sheridan. In the 19th-century West, however, heroes sprang forth seemingly full-blown from the spectacular landscape, a setting previously unavailable to the entire European tradition. Our hero is consistently at his best when depicted in the landscape. Virtually every painting or photograph where the land plays a significant role, portrays a man of considerable dignity if not out and out romance, from John Mix Stanley's *Scouts in the Tetons,* 1860, right up to that venerable icon of advertising, the Marlboro Man. Take him out of this element, or frame him up close or in town and he can shed that dignity like a rattlesnake sheds its skin, as we see in pictures like Olaf Seltzer's *A Dude's Welcome,* 1909, and finally in Andy Warhol's *Double Elvis,* 1963, where the "landscape" has been all but symbolically annihilated by the silver field of the diptych.

So, the essays in the book separate into our two primary areas of inquiry, landscape and hero. I will act as humble guide to the earliest wonders of our imagistic foundation through the work of George Catlin, Karl Bodmer, and Alfred Jacob Miller. Arizona photographer Mark Klett will discuss the challenge an artist faces in working within the myth and tradition of landscape photography. University of Victoria historian Brian Dippie will present Frederic Remington's role in identifying the quintessential western hero. Paul Fees, senior curator of the Buffalo Bill Historical Center in Cody, Wyoming, will make a strong case for the forces that produced that embodiment of legend, Buffalo Bill. Finally, Seattle film critic Kathleen Murphy will explore the western myth in the context of the movies. We feel there are many stories to be told, but that these are at least among the most essential, that without these pieces our ongoing fascination with the puzzle of the West would certainly be diminished, and they shed light on other parts.

• Jesse James with brother, Frank.
Denver Public Library, Western History Department.

We will concentrate on the history of painted images of the West, but also give strong play to photography and film. Photography is not separate from painting, but it functions as a parallel art form, "based not on synthesis but on selection."[2] A single photograph is as much a fiction as a painting—one moment taken to represent many—and yet the best ones ring with recognition. Would any of us be surprised to learn that someone we know is in Joel Sternfeld's *Phoenix, Arizona, August 1979*? If selection is the key there is also a certain synthesis of vision that acts as a collective (photographic) memory: who among us, for instance, has ever seen Yosemite without a wink of an eye from Ansel Adams?

We asked Mark Klett to advise us on particular photographers and images that deal with landscape in order to get the perspective of an artist who works fully conscious of history. If early paintings (ca. 1820-1855) like those of Samuel Seymour, George Catlin, Karl Bodmer, Alfred Jacob Miller, John James Audubon, and the expedition work of John Mix Stanley, all served as "evidence" of America's vast frontier, then the photography that followed a generation later (ca. 1865-1890) served as "proof." William Henry Jackson, Timothy O'Sullivan, William Bell, Carleton Watkins, and others took the developing technology—so recently used to show the horrors of the Civil War—to the wonders of the West and demonstrated an unarguable proof of America's geographic treasures. Later, photography would serve another, social function: to prove the life and death of gunslingers. But this work never developed into the art form landscape photography has, and so our focus will be on these great images that keep our horizons alive.

As an extension of photography, we must admit to the inescapable influence of the movies in perpetuating our fascination with things western. Western films underscore the implicit narrative in most western art, but there is something more fundamental to the role of moving pictures. By the 20th century, the experience of landscape had gotten incorporated into the *fact* of the movies, for the movie screen had become in many ways our culture's most commonly shared environment. If there was an actual landscape it was, to paraphrase Los Angeles film critic Michael Ventura, "God's own backlot."[3]

In the 20th century, movie technology shifts our hero's relationship with the landscape from one where he "enjoys the willful mastery of space that befits an archetype,"[4] to being more about the basic mythmaking magic of the big screen. Mythology scholar Joseph Campbell identified this new space of technology and light in these terms: "The person you are looking at is also somewhere else at the same time. That is the condition of the god."[5] Without that magic our lively interest in the 19th-century art of the West might well be held more as another interesting tangent to European art history, rather than the emblematic image of a national identity that it is today. In the bicentennial year of 1976, Roy Rogers went as far as saying that Western movies are "the only way children today actually have to learn about the winning of the West."[6] He would have been more accurate to say, "the winning of the *myth*," and thereby avoided confusing reality and fantasy. But even there he would have fallen short, for before the movies was painting, photography, fiction, and Buffalo Bill—all of which built on history for their own created dramas. Scenes from Remington and Russell show up full-blown in moving pictures. Russell was an adviser to early silent films, and he shared friendships with such Hollywood cowboys as William S. Hart much as he had with those in Montana.

George Catlin
Eagle Dance. **1845-48**
Oil on canvas
25⅛ x 32⅝ in
National Museum of American Art, Smithsonian
Institution, Gift of Mrs. Joseph Harrison, Jr.

14

John Mix Stanley
Scouts in the Tetons. n.d.
Oil on canvas
24 x 34⅛ in
The Thomas Gilcrease Institute of American History
and Art, Tulsa, Oklahoma.

What we will see in these essays is that the myth of the West is composed of equal parts fact and fiction, and that it depends on both for its durability. We should say here that the myth is that which includes it all, and it is being built all the time from this great bubbling stew of hard evidence and wishful invention. I have been told that this book should be called "Myths of the West," but there is one that most clearly predominates. Our primary national myth is that of an anonymous composite hero who exists as a hero largely because of the landscape he inhabits, who has the power to immunize us against the distractions of his inherent contradictions by exuding a single elusive spirit, and who rematerializes based on the needs of the time.

In Poland's landmark election of 1989, Solidarity's election campaign included a poster picturing Gary Cooper, obviously likening election day to a national High Noon. It worked. But how do millions of Poles know what the image of an actor playing a sheriff in 19th-century western America means? In 1987, Lance Morrow's *Time* magazine essay likened the Oliver North trial to the moral drama of settling the frontier, "the wild places where savages roamed and life was dangerous and action was survival…."[7] How is it, that when we want to explain ourselves best we draw on the West? How is it that any one of us can close our eyes and see Custer forever *about* to die, or describe the vista from the rim of the Grand Canyon, or know how one draws a gun from a holster with great speed and accuracy, even though we may have no firsthand knowledge of these things? In actuality we all begin to answer these questions that call on the past from the perspective and prejudices of now, from the photo of that Solidarity poster, for example, that I saw in *The New York Times* one Sunday. We trace them back through the files of preceding images that help us establish the poster's contemporary identity and meaning.

In the course of organizing this exhibition, I had a wonderful opportunity to perceive this past by visiting such treasure centers of western art as the Amon Carter Museum in Fort Worth, the Buffalo Bill Historical Center in Cody, Wyoming, the Gilcrease Institute in Tulsa, the Museum of Western Art in Denver, the Montana State Historical Society in Helena, the Cowboy Hall of Fame in Oklahoma City, a few rodeos and many other sometimes dusty, sometimes gleaming

Monument Valley in John Ford's
Stagecoach, 1939. Photo courtesy of the
Wisconsin Center for Film and Theater Research.

Joel Sternfeld
Phoenix, Arizona, August, 1979.
Ektacolor print
16 x 20 in
Copyright Joel Sternfeld,
courtesy Pace / MacGill Gallery, New York.

17

outposts where, as they say, "the old West lives on." The amazing thing one discovers at these places is that it does. Museum docents actually hold visitors' attention; visitors look closely at the details of paintings, and talk about them. The past comes alive through the eyes of today, through succeeding filters and somehow there is very little separation, mostly because we don't want there to be. One can go from a 1987 Richard Prince photograph to a 1963 Andy Warhol painting to a 1930 Norman Rockwell, to a 1902 Frederic Remington, to an 1858 Alfred Jacob Miller, barely skipping a beat. Using this "back to the future" view of history we begin the journey with the certainty of having reached the destination: it allows us to ask the question, how did we get here? How did we get to the point where we know what David Halberstam means when he describes baseball great Ted Williams as "crusty, outspoken, and unbending, a frontier man in the modern age, the real John Wayne"?[8] How do we know what "John Wayne" means? How did John Wayne?

After being fairly consumed with the "Myth of the West" over the last three years, I understand how people can spend entire lives trying to grapple with the relatively short history of the American West. The fusion of reality and fantasy drives the desire to sort out its many parts. Few histories have the abundance of such vivid raw material as we find, for example, in the expedition journal of Zenas Leonard, which traced the 1833 trek of Joseph Walker and his company of fifty-eight trappers through unexplored territory from the Rockies to Spanish California. Hardly a fantasist could compete with their reality of having been the first white men (white men love to be "the first white men") to see the spectacles of Yosemite Valley or the giant redwoods, not to mention having their first sighting of the Pacific Ocean coincide exactly with a meteor shower that rocked the entire North American continent.[9] And few historians of other times have had the wondrous side-by-side visual and literary chronicles of a George Catlin (1832-1838) to work with, let alone those parallel paintings and writings of Karl Bodmer and Prince Maximilian (1833-1834) or Alfred Jacob Miller (1837). Then throw in all the geologic surveys and battle reports, tall tales, often spectacular and sometimes suspect works of art, millions upon millions of Mr. Beadle's dime novels and Mr. Grey's paperbacks,

trading ledgers and newspaper accounts, the movies, television shows, advertisements, real daily life lived today—and not a few art books—and you have rich, varied sources of information.

I understand how tempting it is to pull together a comprehensive history of this "perpetual West,"[10] a sort of "imaging" of history. It is, after all, in essence a fairly simple story of forces for or against unlimited freedom.

And yet an accurate overview is impossible, an illusion precisely because each image is an isolated, created "sight-bite" that most often represents the *desire* of history. Even the illusionistic history of the West has its pitfalls, for it is inevitably created out of contradictions. It is at least in part a story of an area and state of mind in conflict with itself for possession of itself, often unable to determine its best side from its worst. Burt Lancaster put it well in the movie *The Professionals:* "Maybe there's only one story. The good guys against the bad guys. Trouble is, who's the good guys?" How can we revel in the glorious self-confidence of the mountain men, the cattle drives, the pioneers, and at the same time know the attendant tragedies that all but destroyed the native cultures? How can we glory in the grandeur of the landscape and still count such burdensome environments as Los Angeles, Phoenix, and Las Vegas as part of the West? But we do, so we can. And we long to get at the heart of it all, again and again.

A couple of years ago my family spent an extraordinarily fine week with the Thomas O'Connors, whose family has been ranching in south Texas for the better part of two centuries. I remember sitting on a corral fence with Michael O'Connor somewhere in the vast, flat rangeland between Goliad and Victoria ("the middle of nowhere") waiting for the trucks that would move the cattle to their summer pasture in northern New Mexico. We were talking about what it takes to run a ranch these days, and he understated the situation exquisitely. "The spirit is the same, but the environment has changed." I knew the environment had changed, but why would the spirit stay the same when nothing else has? What spirit?

I do not want to wax romantic here. The spirit deserves better, for it is much more profound, devilish, deep flowing, insidious, and completely arresting than any cheerleader could implore from a crowd, than any civic booster could tolerate, or any frontier day banner suggest. We will only be able to scratch its rugged and hirsute surface, to identify a few specific areas of inquiry, attempting to pinpoint some of the buiding blocks of America's myth of the West in our exploration into the roots of a national identity.

If we can add anything here, we do it with a respectful irreverence, a willingness to hold up the myth as a mirror that isolates a core image. If we do not see a man with a gun on a horse in a beautiful open landscape, I would like to know what we see instead. "There is more." But he is the one who moves the stories; so much else is the exotic and seductive or real world in which he moves. He is the essence of a society that looked for its challenges from outside its own boundaries, extending frontiers, blazing new trails, conquering dangerous enemies. It is the story of what happens when a social and political impulse based on the primary role of the individual comes in contact with an unprecedented prospect of nature.

In our book's exploration through the fantastic time-travel of imagery, we implicitly face the ghosts of that June day in 1876 on the Little Bighorn: ghosts who would recognize the myth, but not our world. We need to understand the past, but the hardest question we can ask is how this spirit still influences our world.

Chris Bruce
Senior Curator
Henry Art Gallery

With thanks to Joanie Bruce

W SAMO POŁUDNIE
4 CZERWCA 1989

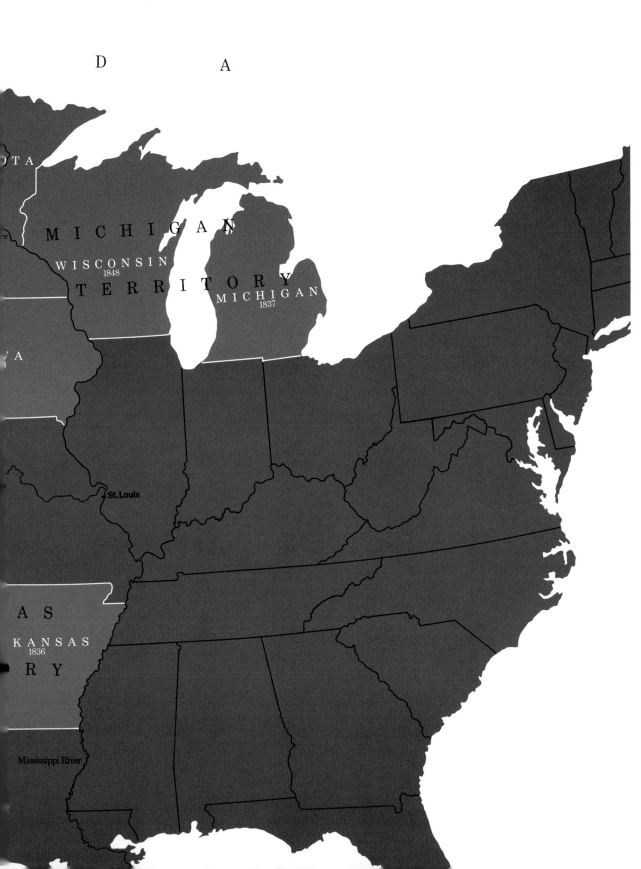

Map of the West

Areas on the map indicate territorial boundaries as of 1821

Astoria, Oregon. Lewis and Clark set up camp for winter, 1805-06

Yellowstone. Solo exploration by John Colter, winter, 1808

Wind River Mountains/Green River area. Rocky Mountain Fur Company holds annual rendezvous, 1825-1840

St. Louis. George Catlin begins his travels up the Missouri River to Ft. Union, March 26, 1832; Karl Bodmer accompanies Prince Maximilian to Ft. McKenzie, April 10, 1833.

Yosemite sited by Joseph Walker's party of 58 trappers during trek from Green River to Monterey, November, 1833

Westport, Missouri. Alfred Jacob Miller accompanies Stewart's party to the rendezvous, April, 1837

"Trail of Tears." Forced relocation of Cherokee nation from Tennessee to Oklahoma, winter, 1838-39

Oregon Trail Survey by John C. Fremont, with Kit Carson as his guide, 1842; 1,000 emigrants use it the following year

Sacramento. Gold discovered at Sutter's Mill, 1848

Wind River Mountains. Albert Bierstadt accompanies Colonel Frederick West Lander's expedition, 1859

St. Joseph, Missouri, to Sacramento. Central Overland Pony Express, April, 1860-October, 1861

Liberty, Missouri. James gang pulls off first day-time bank robbery in history, February 14, 1866

Chisholm Trail opens as primary cattle trail from South Texas to Dodge City and Abilene, Kansas, 1867

Sierra Nevada range. Timothy O'Sullivan accompanies King's Geological Exploration of the 40th Parallel, 1867

Promontory Point, Utah. Transcontinental Railroad joined, May 10, 1869

Yellowstone. William Henry Jackson and Thomas Moran accompany Ferdinand Hayden's Survey, 1871

Willow Creek, Nebraska. While living in San Francisco, Bierstadt arranges for Buffalo Bill to lead buffalo hunt for Russia's Grand Duke Alexis, January, 1872

Yellowstone becomes first national park, March 1, 1872

Grand Canyon. William Bell accompanies Lt. George Wheeler's expedition, 1872

Battle of the Little Bighorn, June 25, 1876

Judith Basin, Montana. Charles Russell arrives from St. Louis, herds sheep before working as a cowboy, 1880

Fort Sumner, New Mexico. Billy the Kid shot by Pat Garrett, July 13, 1881

Tombstone, Arizona. Shootout at OK Corral, October, 1881

North Platte, Nebraska. Buffalo Bill's first Wild West Show, July 4, 1882

Peabody, Kansas. Frederic Remington buys a ranch, 1883

Oklahoma City. Oklahoma Land Rush, April 22, 1889

Wounded Knee Massacre, December 29, 1890

Wilcox, Wyoming. Butch Cassidy and the Wild Bunch rob and dynamite their first train, June 2, 1899.

Hollywood. *Hell's Hinges* filmed by William S. Hart, 1916

Taos. Georgia O'Keeffe's first visit to New Mexico, 1917

Monument Valley. *Stagecoach* filmed by John Ford, 1939

Arizona. *Red River* filmed by Howard Hawks, 1948

Durango, Mexico. *The Wild Bunch* filmed by Sam Peckinpah, 1969

THE WESTERN LANDSCAPE

Thomas Moran. *Cliffs of Green River,* 1874 (detail).
See page 77.

George Catlin
The Author Painting a Chief at the Base of the Rocky Mountains. **1850**
From *A Souvenir of the North American Indians,* vol. 2, plate 102.
Watercolor
19⅛ x 13¼ in
Rare Books and Manuscripts Division, the New York Public Library, Astor, Lenox, and Tilden Foundations.

24

G. Catlin.

The Author painting a Chief at the base of the Rocky Mountains.

Chris Bruce

"History is a message in a bottle, cast about by the tides and currents of image and myth."[1]
William W. Savage, Jr., 1979

25

• **George Catlin**
St. Louis, from the River Below.
1832-33
Oil on canvas
19⅜ x 26⅞ in
National Museum of American Art, Smithsonian Institution, Gift of Mrs. Joseph Harrison, Jr.

The notes for the text begin on page 185.

Maybe he thinks back six years from this spring day in 1832, and he thinks of Philadelphia and the day he first saw the bronzed, painted men from the headwaters of an endless river: men dressed in robes of leather, beads, bone, teeth, and feathers. Maybe he has a memory of that bright city, pulsing in waves of sound and movement at the sensation of such visitors, and he remembers that first perception of his destiny, just as he now tries to focus beyond the shocking sparks of light that reflect off the water hurling by him to the slower procession of bushes and low cliffs that line the river. Maybe he thinks of his wife, and he looks at his hands, permanently stained around the fingertips from painting. They will always be like that, he thinks. Funny that such a simple thing separates him so from others.

He is now on board the steamer *Yellow Stone,* almost nine hundred miles from St. Louis, on its maiden voyage up the Missouri. The Indians call it "Big Medicine Canoe with Eyes" because it seems to see its own way and steer itself.[2] All the way up the river, the Indians have been amazed at the sight. They have, of course, seen the small mechanisms of white culture like guns, timepieces, traps, compasses, but never one so immense in their own territory. Certainly chiefs who have traveled east have returned with stories, but who knows if they were believed, and if they were, how those beliefs were translated into the mind's eye.

Canoes begin to appear, greeting the double-decked paddle-wheeler. The other passengers stir. The painter stands up. There before them on the huge expanse of flat ground surrounding the fort are over six hundred teepees. Canoes now swarm the steamer like mosquitoes as it pulls to shore.

George Catlin had a lot to learn about the potential of his art that spring day in 1832 when he stood on the deck of the *Yellow Stone* and looked out at Fort Pierre, seemingly light years from St. Louis, and a world apart from Philadelphia. Some six thousand Sioux had gathered there for a festival of trade, games, and religious ceremonies, and stayed on to witness the arrival of the "Big Thunder Canoe." Catlin must have thought he had died and gone to heaven. He was beginning his lifelong work on the wonders of the western landscape and its native people, and here before him was the assembled leadership and almost fifteen percent of the entire Sioux nation.

I like to think of Catlin at that moment of time, getting off the boat, eager to set up his makeshift portrait studio. He is less the sometimes bitter authority he would later become; more someone who finds himself with something he has to do, in an environment he *likes*, and is good in. He could paint, with speed and accuracy. Who else out there could paint like that? He could ride a horse like a champion, and shoot. He enjoyed the life; he was—how could it be?—in his element.

One can imagine actually *seeing* the changes taking effect within Catlin as the process of painting takes hold, with all his self-contained intensity meeting such unprecedented, powerful subjects (he knew he was the first, really, to do this). And all that external energy, all those Indians for God's sake, watching him perform, yes, "miracles." His confidence would grow, his insights and perception flow. After a full day of painting, having been transported into the magical realm of his art, this synthesis of an alien universe and the most immediate world of his own hand, he would walk the vast compound of tents, fires, races, dances. He was meeting his mission in life, seeing beyond art-making. He had been somewhere else all day, deep inside his imagined Indian world, beginning to understand it, beginning to *love* it.

Catlin would go on to wander the West for parts of eight years, and he would also see evidence of another world that exploited and subjected the native people; he would write about that world and rail against it, but he would not paint it. Now however, at Fort Pierre in 1832, not yet fully conscious of that other world, he was a miracle worker, and the prospect of his painting was still so heady. "To these people, the operations of my brush were entirely new and unaccountable, and excited amongst them the greatest curiosity imaginable."[3] They had never seen representational portraiture being made, and he was given the distinguished title of *Ee-cha-zoo-kah-ga-wa-kon*, the Medicine Painter.

He painted a number of frontal portraits at Fort Pierre, enthusiastically received by this audience. And then he painted an untypical profile of one "noble fine fellow" named *Mah-to-tchee-ga*, the Little Bear, a chief of the Hunkpapa Sioux. Today it stands as one among many hundreds of Catlin's portraits, but on that day it signaled one of the strangest events in any artist's career. Suddenly the buoyant collective mood shifted to dark as a rival chief of the Bad Arrow Points band known as *Shon-ka*, the Dog, "an ill-natured and surly man despised by the chief of every other band," began to taunt Little Bear as "but half a man," using Catlin's picture as proof. It is a well-known story of lesser men calling out more respected men to build a macho reputation, complete with desperately concerned wife and family. The upshot is that Little Bear, pride on the line, stands up to the Dog, but gets his face blown half-away in the ensuing shuffle, "carrying away one half of the jaws, and the flesh from the nostrils and corner of the mouth, to the ear, including one eye, and leaving the jugular vein entirely exposed"—the

George Catlin
Little Bear, A Hunkpapa Brave. **1832**
Oil on canvas
29 x 24 in
National Museum of American Art, Smithsonian Institution, Gift of Mrs. Joseph Harrison, Jr.

half Catlin did not paint.[4] He dies the next day, amidst wailing cries
of grief and anger.

The Dog and his small group make their getaway, and the
revenge story takes over as Little Bear's tribe makes plans to avenge
their fallen brother's death. Catlin quickly begins to make his own plans,
for he is clearly implicated and the eyes of vengeance have now turned
toward him as well. His "medicine is too great!" He made his portraits
"alive…and he can trouble their spirits when they are dead!"[5] How
quickly things could change. His escape is arranged expeditiously by
Mr. Laidlaw of the American Fur Company, and four months later, blood
still running hot, Catlin and his companions had to make their way
undercover, downriver past a Sioux village.

Catlin's story, told by Catlin in his *Letters and Notes on the
Manners, Customs, and Condition of the North American Indians*,
published in 1841, emphasizes not only how alien the tradition of European painting was to the native people of the West, but also indicates
the role of the artist in presenting the life of these little-known territories
to eastern audiences; part visual interpreter, part scientific recorder,
but also part storyteller. How strange and magical the land beyond the
Mississippi must have seemed in the 1830s, and how tantalizing each
new report of America's vast new resources must have been.

No art genre is more consistently confused with historical
record than the art of the West, primarily because the first painters—and
a generation later, the first photographers—went west in various documentary capacities, largely responding to this obvious void in the visual
record. Artists are always hungry for fresh subject matter, and in 1830
the West was a huge untapped artistic opportunity already charged with
fantastic literary associations, from the journals of Lewis and Clark,
Zebulon Pike, and Stephen Long to the fictions of James Fenimore
Cooper and Timothy Flint. Alfred Jacob Miller would admonish artists
to forget about Greece and Egypt and go West: "Here is a new field…
that has been waiting…for thousands of years."[6] The written reports
had "satisfied desire and created desire: the desire of a westering nation,"
adding scattered details to an overall mystery.[7]

George Catlin
Fort Pierre, Mouth of the Teton River,
1,200 Miles Above St. Louis. **1832**
Oil on canvas
11¼ x 14½ in
National Museum of American Art, Smithsonian
Institution, Gift of Mrs. Joseph Harrison, Jr.

The artists provided a visualization of this mysterious realm, "proof" the mind could catch hold of. As difficult as it is for us to comprehend, their work was depicted on a previously clean slate, the first pictorial evidence not only of remarkable landscapes, but of wild and stunning human and animal life. The viewing experience of the 19th-century audience was, in many ways, more drastic than our own glimpse of Mars or Neptune via *Voyager* satellite. In considering this idea of evidence we now have the luxury of hindsight, personal experience, and photography. But to the men and women of the eastern seaboard and Europe circa 1840, the fresh visual records of George Catlin (1796-1872), Karl Bodmer (1809-1883), and Alfred Jacob Miller (1810-1874) must have been wondrously confusing, like mythology scholar Joseph Campbell's descriptive essence of myth: an unleashing of strange "vapors, odd beings, terrors, and deluding images [where] not only jewels but dangerous jinn abide…that carry keys that open the whole realm of the desired and feared adventure of the discovery of the self."[8] Eastern audiences were hungry to receive the evidence of who, what, and where the West was, but there was also a larger mystery only the most visionary could then foresee: that of an emerging American identity. This is the mystery that would begin to be pieced together by these three artists.

If the western myth "tells us what happened when ordinary people moved into an extraordinary land,"[9] then the artists were no exception. Catlin, Bodmer and Miller returned east with evidence of the West observed firsthand between 1832 and 1838, a time when Catlin could visit a Comanche village and still be "looked upon with as much curiosity as if he had come from the moon."[10] These artists crossed the threshold of adventure into unknown regions and brought back full mystic chalices of evidence of a new unimaginable world to the people on both sides of the Atlantic. But these are impure documents, all *based* on fact, but not fact.

It is well to remember that the artist's hand interpreted the land since the links of western imagery to history are always so strong. A sense of purpose — a desire to find what one was looking for — combined with the artists' own abilities and personal styles to create images that functioned partly as art and largely as the pieces of an overall puzzle of a little-known land of radical extremes. The artists venture beyond the great plains with wonderful assortments of baggage: they will make choices about what to document and *for whom* that result in a diversity of imagery, one West composed of many parts.

If we wanted to invent a visual foundation for this composite of fiction and history that our culture would soon take to heart, we could hardly have done better than the spectacular and diverse bodies of work of George Catlin, Karl Bodmer, and Alfred Jacob Miller. Their work seen together (about one thousand separate images, most duplicated several times) combines an exotic but realistic setting (Bodmer), with romantic idealism (Miller), as well as the identification of a vast surreal arena that includes equal portions of wonder and danger (Catlin).

All three artists set out from the rambunctious river town of St. Louis between 1832 and 1837, a full three decades after Lewis and Clark's remarkably sensitive and well-organized expedition (1804-1806), which covered more than five thousand miles with hardly a hint of conflict with the numerous native cultures they encountered. It was the prospect of this expedition that encouraged President Thomas Jefferson to suggest in 1804 that the land west of the Mississippi be set aside for fifty years as a preserve.[11] Fat chance. By the 1830s, the West had undergone changes unprecedented in the entire history of human beings in the region, largely through the mad drive to capitalize on the rich natural resources suddenly owned by the United States of America. The artists of the 19th century would confront a West in a state of radical flux, but which could also display its timeless wild purity at any given turn of the trail. In fact it was a wildness that attracted wildness that drove the reckless exploitation, as America's vanguard in the West was, for better or worse, the trapper, the trader, and the forts established by the fur companies.

Karl Bodmer
Banks of the Missouri. **1833**
Watercolor on paper
7 7⁄8 x 12 1⁄8 in
Joslyn Art Museum, Omaha, Nebraska;
Gift of Enron Art Foundation.

30

St. Louis was the "edge," the jumping-off place, a city with an official population of about sixteen thousand in 1840. It was a frontier case study in contrasts, where millions of dollars in beaver skins had been unloaded in the previous two decades: a place of elegant mansions, rampant crime, no police force, three newspapers, no paved streets, and plenty of taverns.[12] Its most prominent citizen must have been General William Clark, at sixty the surviving co-leader of the expedition that opened the West. He built a large residence in 1818, which included a room one hundred feet by thirty-five feet that housed his collection of Indian artifacts. A visit with Clark before heading west was both an homage to the great trailblazer and a source of practical information. Catlin, Bodmer, and Miller made the pilgrimage, and each came away with encouragement.

There are odd and intriguing parallels between these artists. Catlin, beginning in 1832, and Bodmer in 1833, covered much the same territory, each going up the Missouri aboard the newly commissioned steamer *Yellow Stone*. Both artists made formal portraits of the Indians, painted the wonders of their customs and land, and both chose to delete the fur traders and other white interlopers (except for occasionally including themselves) from their pictorial records as being beneath their artistic missions. Both artists also witnessed the Mandan who were then supposed to have been descendants of ancient Welsh explorers and who would by 1838 be virtually wiped out by smallpox. Their styles however are markedly different: Catlin's primitive and surreal, Bodmer's exquisitely realistic. Miller and Bodmer had equally distinct styles, but shared other similarities as both were trained in Europe, went west only once, both in the employ of European noblemen—though for quite different reasons. Their stories are familiar to many, but they illustrate a fascinating and often contradictory combination of motives that create the visual underpinnings of the myth of the West. Though Catlin was the first to head west, we will begin with Bodmer because his paintings actually reached a wide general audience a year before Catlin's. Furthermore, Bodmer's were stylistically the most realistic, thus encouraging the belief that art could portray the West accurately.

Karl Bodmer

Twenty-three-year-old, Zurich-trained Karl Bodmer came to America in 1832 in the company of Prince Alexander Philipp Maximilian of Germany and his manservant David Dreidoppel to explore and record the North American wilderness. Maximilian had previously explored South America and had just spent the past ten years cataloging its flora and fauna. He was a man western historian William H. Goetzmann describes as one who "put his Enlightenment training in the exact sciences to the service of a romantic world view that was fascinated by the remote and exotic."[13] He also had the good sense to bring Bodmer along to provide illustrations for his North American atlas. When they arrived in St. Louis in the spring of 1833, the trio's high expectations could be excused for beginning to fade, for the previous eight months' travel had barely offered a clue as to the majestic wild America they had hoped to find. But in St. Louis they saw their first western Indians, and General Clark's tales certainly must have rekindled their hopes. Here they also saw some of George Catlin's paintings, and though we do not know the exact pictures, it is interesting to imagine how the more competent Swiss artist reacted to these works. There are similarities in many of their works, and in each case Bodmer goes Catlin one better in terms of composition and technical achievements. If nothing else, they prepared the vision and fueled the Europeans' enthusiasm for the upcoming yearlong adventure.

On April 10, 1833, having added an interpreter to their small party (Sacajawea's husband Toussaint Charbonneau), they set out up the Missouri and ran into the worst storm any of them had ever seen. The *Yellow Stone* would be almost crippled by the time they reached present-day Kansas City, but they would press on more than two thousand miles upriver as far as Fort McKenzie near the mouth of the Marias River in the heart of territory controlled by the fierce Blackfoot. They would travel through natural wonders of lush wildlife as well as the strange, monumental landscape of the Mauvaises Terres (the badlands along the upper Missouri in present-day North Dakota), where Maximilian would report, "the silence of the bare, dead, lonely wilderness is but seldom interrupted by the howling of wolves, the bellowing of buffalo, or the screaming of crows."[14] They would come upon huge encampments of Indians, sometimes thousands strong. At Fort McKenzie Bodmer would have the distinction of being the only artist to witness a ferocious battle between tribes of Blackfoot and Assiniboin. Originally the prince had planned to winter in the wilderness and move on into the Rockies. But faced with hostile Indians, lack of interpreters and supplies, they would keelboat back downriver five hundred miles from Fort McKenzie and spend the entire frigid winter at the more primitive Fort Clark (near present-day

Karl Bodmer
Rock Formations on the Upper Missouri. **1833**
Watercolor on paper
12½ x 7¾ in
Joslyn Art Museum, Omaha, Nebraska;
Gift of Enron Art Foundation.

Bismarck, North Dakota). Here Bodmer painted such works as *View of the Mandan Village Mih-Tutta-Hang-Kush Near Fort Clark*, 1834, in temperatures that sometimes froze his paint, amidst the soon to be extinct Mandan.[15] By April 1834, the river thawed, they would begin their return to St. Louis with an overall treasury of adventures and stunning pictures for publication in *Maximilian's Travels in the Interior of North America in the Years 1832 to 1834*. By mid-July, they were on the boat back to Europe, never to return to North America.

Of all the artists who have painted the West, Bodmer's work is the most immediately believable because of its precise draftsmanship. It is "photographic" before there was photography, although there was an interpretive selection process at work here that omitted the seamier newcomers to the West: the trappers, buffalo hunters, common servants, etc. Interestingly, some of the "action scenes" such as the battle at Fort McKenzie and the awesome *Bison Dance of the Mandan Indians*, ca. 1839-1843 would not be painted until he returned to Europe. Their mission in America was ostensibly a more "scientific" cataloging of native types rather than the creation of a narrative. But by their return Bodmer and his patron Maximilian must have realized that these unique events fairly cried out for visual representation. Paintings Bodmer made in America and Europe would first dazzle visitors to the Paris Exhibition of 1836 and present an apparently objective portrait of a western wonderland. These works established a foundation of spectacular evidence of extravagant land forms, monumental in shape and scale, inhabited by teeming animal life and wild, beautiful people. Bodmer's paintings were as utterly believable as they were what the audience wanted to believe.

• Karl Bodmer
View of the Mandan Village Mih-
Tutta-Hang-Kush Near Fort Clark.
1834
Watercolor on paper
11¼ x 16⅝ in
Joslyn Art Museum, Omaha, Nebraska;
Gift of Enron Art Foundation.

After Karl Bodmer
Bison Dance of the Mandan Indians.
1839-43
Engraving with aquatint (handcolored)
on paper
18⅛ x 24¾ in
Joslyn Art Museum, Omaha, Nebraska;
Gift of Enron Art Foundation.

Alfred Jacob Miller

From Bodmer's exquisite precision, we turn to Alfred Jacob Miller's work, which strays from pictorial accuracy, and expands the visual West to something of an American Camelot full of splendid personages. Miller was a Baltimore native trained at the Ecole des Beaux-Arts in Paris in 1833-1834 under the pervasive influence of French Romanticism as most fully represented by Eugène Delacroix. Miller's call to the West came in the spring of 1837 soon after the twenty-seven-year-old artist opened his studio over L. Chittenden's dry goods store on Chartres Street in the French Quarter of New Orleans. A tall, erect gentleman with a hook nose (who Miller thought was a Kentuckian because of his stylish dress) appeared, looked around, and complimented Miller on his paintings.[16] A few days later this Scottish nobleman, Captain William Drummond Stewart, returned and made the invitation that would change Miller's life and create the only firsthand picture we have of an important chapter in the history of the West. Miller's job would be to serve as expedition artist to the rendezvous of the mountain men, that annual gathering of trade, supply, and debauchery of the fur trappers and their coterie. And, along the way, portray Captain Stewart as one dashing figure among many.

One can hardly imagine the thoughts that went through the unathletic young artist's mind as he contemplated the prospect of a demanding fifteen-hundred-mile trek over partially unmapped territory from St. Louis to the interior of the Rocky Mountains. But he was there at Westport station (present-day Kansas City) at the end of April as the caravan of forty-five men completed their elaborate outfitting. The estimated cost to Stewart was about $23,000 and included twenty carts full of supplies as extravagant as tins of sardines, fine whiskey, and a grand striped tent complete with Oriental rugs, all guaranteed to uphold Stewart's reputation among such legendary men of the mountains as Kit Carson, Jim Bridger, and Joseph Walker.[17] As we see in Miller's *Prairie Scene: Mirage,* 1858-60, they headed northwest across the prairies through places that read like a poem of the plains: Chimney Rock, Scott's Bluffs, Fort Laramie, Independence Rock, and Devil's Gate along the Sweetwater River, the entryway to the Rockies. From there they would journey through South Pass to the Big Sandy and into the Wind River Mountains to the rendezvous site on Horse Creek near the Upper Green River. A member of the expedition would recount the first sighting: "We came suddenly upon a long line of beautiful Indian tents ranging in regular order, and stretching away for at least two miles in perspective, and terminating in a wide and circular array of the same romantic and fairy-looking dwellings."[18]

If Bodmer set the standard for a studied depiction of the land and Native American, Miller certainly set the paradigm for a romantic interpretation of the West and its Anglo-American hero. It is ironic that Miller was the only artist to see the rugged mountain man in his element, and the fact that he could shower what must have been something of a 19th-century equivalent of the Hell's Angels with such a romantic glow only proves how powerful an artistic vision is in creating a picture of the West. Such works as *Antoine Watering Stewart's Horse,* n.d. provide future artists with a model western hero, for Miller's paintings are nothing if not lovely portraits of benign fur trappers, peacefully plying their trade in a misty natural paradise framed by forest and mountains, or enjoying the idyllic pleasures of the rendezvous.* Of course, the buckskin-clad Stewart astride his milk-white charger only helps tip the scales of heroic type. Others have been less enchanted with this rustic hero, noting that the mountain men as a group were probably "as sensitive as deer to the charms of scenery, possessing warlike skills, practical cunning and sheer ferocity as developed to the highest degree."[19]

But Miller was simply taking his own artistic predisposition to the annual mountain bazaar. He was flush with his European training and completely encouraged by the cultivated and adventure-loving Captain Stewart, not only during the journey to the rendezvous, but later when the artist set up a studio to make finished oils from his field paintings at his patron's family estate at Murthly Castle in Perthshire, Scotland (1840-1842). Miller wrote to his brother in 1841 that the lord of the manor felt perfectly at home in "offering criticism on any point wherein he thinks I may be wrong and woe to the Indian which has not sufficient dignity in expression or carriage, for out he must come!"[20]

Some of Miller's paintings are reconstructions of Stewart's stories about himself like the chivalric *Attack by Crow Indians,* ca. 1858-1860, never actually witnessed by the artist at all, and yet these works were often exhibited side by side with others that were more factual documents of the expedition. Though the six months with Stewart would be Miller's only trip west, future patrons would request duplications of these field sketches. So the art of Alfred Jacob Miller would continue to be the west of 1837 until his death in 1874, a West of "the deep purple masses…salmon colored rock, immense sheets of clear water…as fresh and beautiful as if just from the hand of the Creator."[21]

While the lack of strict realism in Miller's body of work demonstrates the difficulty the public had in determining an accurate picture of the fur trade, his paintings do convey a dominant artistic and philosophic sensibility which idealized wilderness and which would reach its penultimate expression in the writings of Thoreau and Whitman in the 1840s. Miller could at once state, "Only in savage life [does] real and absolute liberty exist," while at the same time make pictures not of savagery at all, but of a refined elegance in a new costume and setting.[22] Whatever controversy there is concerning the detailed characteristics of Miller's mountain man—and by implication, the western hero in general— all would agree that the notion of men living out an allegiance to wild freedom is one of the West's most absolute ideals. Although he painted many Indian pictures, he did so within the context of Sir Stewart's adventure, and thus shifts our focus from the exotic lure of the native to the romantic glow of the white man gone natural.

*For further information on the Rendezvous, see page 54.

Alfred Jacob Miller
Prairie Scene: Mirage. **1858-60**
Watercolor on paper
8$\frac{13}{16}$ x 13$\frac{3}{16}$ in
The Walters Art Gallery, Baltimore, Maryland.

Alfred Jacob Miller
Green River (Oregon). **1858-60**
Watercolor on paper
9¹⁄₁₆ x 12¼ in
The Walters Art Gallery, Baltimore, Maryland.

George Catlin
Buffalo Chase, Mouth of the
Yellowstone. **1832-33**
Oil on canvas
24 x 29 in
National Museum of American Art, Smithsonian
Institution, Gift of Mrs. Joseph Harrison, Jr.

38

George Catlin

As significant as Bodmer's and Miller's contributions were, it is George Catlin who ultimately commands our attention, for only Catlin freely made the West his true calling. His extensive writings go far beyond hired document to a strong opinion that the native population was doomed, a position that dramatically inserts the idea of right and wrong into the developing western story. He had no particular patronage to please, and he arrived in St. Louis in 1830, determined to leave a profound personal record of the Native American. He took his first trip up the Missouri on March 26, 1832, and in the next six years would travel all over America visiting as many as 146 tribes in all.[23]

There could hardly be a document of greater conscience or farsightedness than his *Letters and Notes on the Manners, Customs, and Condition of the North American Indians*. For while others worked well within the going perceptions of their own time, Catlin managed to consider cause and effect, as well as the heritage and future ramifications of the present mixing of cultural forces in the West. He could see a day coming that would need his work as a reminder of what was lost in our headlong dash across the continent. His great insight was that this environment was *not* "safe:" it was not Eden or Camelot, nor a place of clinical study, although it held those prospects. There are snakes, fires, monsters, and the destructive forces of American free enterprise, as well as sylvan fields in Catlin's West.

His written and visual record is complex, and includes stirring accounts any raconteur would be proud to call his own, tempting the reader by announcing, "Now for medecines [sic] or mysteries—for doctors, high priests, for hocus pocus, witchcraft, and animal magnetism!"[24] He could be swept away by the "soul melting scenery that was about me!…A place where a Divine would confess that he never had fancied Paradise…."[25] But his "heart has bled with pity,"[26] and his primary agenda was founded on his observation of the native people "that so long as the past and present system of trade and whiskey-selling is tolerated amongst them, there is little hope for their improvement, nor any chance for more than a temporary life."[27]

To see Catlin's work fully, to understand the cultural loss these images assert, one must also read his text. Indeed, even the fate of his paintings fell victim to the inability of the United States government to come to productive terms with native peoples. In 1838 Jefferson Davis shot down a Senate proposal to buy Catlin's pictures. Davis was, in fact, the very person who had proposed their purchase a year earlier. Yet by 1838, President Andrew Jackson's Indian policy had removed the southern tribes beyond the Mississippi, in Catlin's own words, "twelve and fourteen hundred miles West, to a wild and lawless region, where their wants are to be supplied by the traders…who are daily and hourly selling whiskey and rum, and senseless gewgaws…with guns and other instruments of death, unthought of by the simple savage."[28] Catlin obviously does not hold back his outcry, and the government wanted no evidence that would enlist sympathy or gain understanding for the Indian situation.

Catlin would take his paintings and concerns to Europe in 1839, not returning to the United States until 1870, two years before his death. We can begin to comprehend what was lost in the Senate's discouragement of Catlin by remembering what was gained when the government paid attention to the work of two other artists. For in 1872, Thomas Moran's paintings and William Henry Jackson's photographs would play a huge role in the formation of the national park system. One can only speculate on the contributions Catlin might have made to our understanding and appreciation of the West if he had been given the green light. Was he so out of sync, so far ahead of his time? Certainly, the "Trail of Tears" was not something an expanding nation wanted to dwell on, but more realistically, it would simply take years to create the national awareness that would understand the need to preserve a resource like Yellowstone let alone the riches of native cultures. In 1839, there was the barest glimmer of a western legacy. There was only an intense curiosity and an imagined sense of western possibilities, as yet uninfluenced by the layers of information artists like Catlin, Bodmer, Miller, and others would add in abundance in succeeding years.

Catlin's most general conception of the West can be seen in terms of a vast morality play at a time when Manifest Destiny called most of his fellow countrymen. His final chapter in *Letters and Notes* is "an unrequited account of sin and injustice" of the government and fur companies against the native population.[29] He sees these unhappy consequences as an unfortunate essence of European/American character: Greed. His book is also a remarkable defense and detailed cataloging of the native cultures as legitimate, noble, and moral, on their own terms in their own environment. A free, sketchy painting such as *Buffalo Chase, Mouth of the Yellowstone*, 1832-33 acts as an example of the spectacular and worthy existence that is being destroyed.

George Catlin
*Medicine Man Performing His
Mysteries Over a Dying Man.* **1832**
Oil on canvas
29 x 24 in
National Museum of American Art, Smithsonian
Institution, Gift of Mrs. Joseph Harrison, Jr.

40

In turning his eye from pure observation or an exercise in artistic style to a reflection on the ramifications of the building clash between opposing cultures, Catlin becomes part of the turn the West makes toward a place where the dramas of good and evil will be played out for America. His writings present a strong case on the source of the conflict that will fuel the western story for at least another half-century, while his paintings present a lyric wildness.

Catlin sets up a sort of ironic subtradition within western art in which the artist sees the loss, mourns its passing, and yet does so with vital, even rousing works of art. Other artists also will note the losses not so apparent in the bulk of their pictures, so in that sense the images become treasures of treasures lost—all the more precious. Artists as closely associated with an overtly idealized West as John Mix Stanley, Albert Bierstadt, Frederic Remington, and Charles Russell will acknowledge the losses in words, and they will continue to make spectacular images that glorify the glorious West that was. They will however, also make visual statements directed precisely at the loss.

While Catlin's combined writings and paintings may be the greatest humanistic achievement of our three artists, he could not have created this mythic base alone, for in execution his work is primitive and in message his writings are at times overbearing. They could easily have been considered the righteous mission of an obsessive eccentric. In fact, if we had been left with only one of any of these artists, the foundation imagery of the art of the West would have led to a vastly different development of our myth—or even no cultural myth at all. What if we had Bodmer's record alone? We would have been left with more of an impulse for descriptive fact, a West of observation for the naturalist or anthropologist. If Miller alone, we could have soon been lost in a too dreamy ideal world that certainly would have reached an early dead-end. Or even more hypothetically, what if Catlin had painted as a social critic, showing the process of destruction rather than recording the positive scenes about to be lost? Yet if these three bodies of work are put together, we have not only a composite evidence of what was or might have been, but also the foundation of an epic drama comprised of three specific and necessary ingredients that combine historic facts with inspired telling: Bodmer's believable and dignified setting, Miller's romantic heroic ideal, and Catlin's primal environment under the dark cloud of cultural conflict. Given this visual foundation, the West will continue to be seen in terms of a cohabitation for unrestricted freedom, exotic adventure, wild exploitation, and spectacular beauty.

In attempting to get behind the images to some larger issues of content we face the same problem Catlin and his followers faced: the pictures themselves have an emblematic fascination and power more far-reaching than any written analysis or narrative. If, as novelist Umberto Eco says, "Images are the literature of the layman," then we are all laymen.[30] It is our dilemma that these images are bright, wonderful, entertaining, and can represent something so entirely independent of certain harder consequential realities of which we are all aware.

Yet in the exploration for meaning, these pictures take on a complexity and resonance that give us pause. That we can now stand on the Oregon coast, where Lewis and Clark wintered in 1805, and wonder at the fate of the ocean at our feet means that we are all in the position Catlin realized for himself: awed by the many gifts of our western heritage, but aware of a chilling future that awaits if we do not attend to the many signs of abuse. Catlin, Bodmer, and Miller all present art that is close to evidence, but that is perhaps ultimately a force in the service of myth, which not only has the ability to combine seemingly contradictory elements into one whole, but also to blow in from the past and shake the conscience of the present.

Chris Bruce is senior curator at the Henry Art Gallery, University of Washington. He has written primarily on issues in contemporary American art and has organized such exhibitions as *History of Photography; No: Contemporary American Dada; Louise Bourgeois: Works 1943-1987;* and *Sources of Light: Contemporary American Luminism.*

George Catlin
Prairie Bluffs Burning. **1832**
Oil on canvas
11¼ x 14½ in
National Museum of American Art, Smithsonian
Institution, Gift of Mrs. Joseph Harrison, Jr.

42

George Catlin
"Brick Kilns," Clay Bluffs, 1,900 Miles Above St. Louis. 1832
Oil on canvas
11¼ x 14⅜ in
National Museum of American Art, Smithsonian Institution, Gift of Mrs. Joseph Harrison, Jr.

George Catlin
The Rattlesnakes Den, Fountain of Poison. n.d.
Oil on canvas
18 x 26¾ in
The Thomas Gilcrease Institute of American History and Art, Tulsa, Oklahoma.

George Catlin
Buffalo Herds Crossing the Upper Missouri. 1832
Oil on canvas
11¼ x 14½ in
National Museum of American Art, Smithsonian Institution, Gift of Mrs. Joseph Harrison, Jr.

George Catlin
Buffalos (Bulls and Cows) Grazing in the Prairie. c. 1855-70
Oil on cardboard on Bristol board
18⅝ x 24⅞ in
Courtesy of the Buffalo Bill Historical Center, Cody, Wyoming.

George Catlin
An "Oak Opening," Mouth of the Platte, with a Party of Indians Playing on Horseback. c. 1855-70
Oil on cardboard on Bristol board
17⅞ x 24½ in
Courtesy of the Buffalo Bill Historical Center, Cody, Wyoming.

George Catlin
Mouth of the Platte River,
900 Miles Above St. Louis. **1832**
Oil on canvas
11¼ x 14½ in
National Museum of American Art, Smithsonian
Institution, Gift of Mrs. Joseph Harrison, Jr.

45

Karl Bodmer
Mouth of the Platte River. 1833
Watercolor and pencil on paper
10⅝ x 16⅝ in

Joslyn Art Museum, Omaha, Nebraska;
Gift of Enron Art Foundation.

46

After Karl Bodmer
View of the Bear Paw Mountains
from Fort McKenzie. **1833**
Watercolor on paper
11½ x 16⅜ in
Joslyn Art Museum, Omaha, Nebraska;
Gift of Enron Art Foundation.

Karl Bodmer
Buffalo and Elk on the Upper Missouri.
1833
Watercolor on paper
9¾ x 12¼ in
Joslyn Art Museum, Omaha, Nebraska;
Gift of Enron Art Foundation.

Karl Bodmer
Fort Union on the Missouri. **n.d.**
Handcolored engraving with aquatint
9⅝ x 12⅜ in
Joslyn Art Museum, Omaha, Nebraska

Karl Bodmer
Unusual Elevations on the Upper Missouri. n.d.
Watercolor over pencil on paper
12⅛ x 7⅝ in
Joslyn Art Museum, Omaha, Nebraska;
Gift of Enron Art Foundation.

Karl Bodmer
Unusual Sandstone Formations on the Upper Missouri. 1833
Watercolor on paper
7⅞ x 12½ in
Joslyn Art Museum, Omaha, Nebraska;
Gift of Enron Art Foundation.

49

• **Karl Bodmer**
Noapéh (Troop of Soldiers),
Assiniboin Man. **1833**
Watercolor and pencil on paper
17 x 11⅞ in
Joslyn Art Museum, Omaha, Nebraska;
Gift of Enron Art Foundation.

50

Alfred Jacob Miller
Attack by Crow Indians. **1858-60**
Watercolor on paper
9⅞ x 13⅝ in
The Walters Art Gallery, Baltimore, Maryland.

Alfred Jacob Miller
Yell of Triumph. **1858-60**
Watercolor on paper
8⅛ x 12⁷⁄₁₆ in
The Walters Art Gallery, Baltimore, Maryland.

Alfred Jacob Miller
*Crossing the River, Trapper Trying Its
Depth.* 1858-60
Watercolor on paper
8¾ x 12⁵⁄₁₆ in
The Walters Art Gallery, Baltimore, Maryland.

Alfred Jacob Miller
Buffalo Chase—by a Female. 1858-60
Watercolor on paper
8⅞ x 12¼ in
The Walters Art Gallery, Baltimore, Maryland.

Alfred Jacob Miller
The Lost Greenhorn. n.d.
Oil on canvas
17⅞ x 23⅞ in
Courtesy of the Buffalo Bill Historical Center,
Cody, Wyoming.

53

This painting is based on the adventure of John, the English
cook of Captain William Stewart's expedition to the 1837
rendezvous. When John boasted that he could bag his own
buffalo, he was given the opportunity and sent out to hunt
alone. But when he did not return to camp after the second
day, the caravan commander sent the hunters out to find
him. They brought back an embarrassed cook who had lost
his way, was very hungry, and found himself in the path of a
stampeding herd of buffalo.

The Mountain Man's Rendezvous, 1825-1840

The annual summer rendezvous was the most significant social and business event of the American fur trade that evolved during the 1820s and 1830s on the western slope of the Rocky Mountains. It began in July 1825, when William Ashley, founder of the Rocky Mountain Fur Company, met his men as planned at Henry's Fork of the Green River to pick up pelts, pay the trappers, and resupply them for the next season. From then on, rendezvous were held at various locations around the confluence of the present-day borders of Idaho, Utah, and Wyoming. The event quickly grew into a bizarre and profane celebration that stood in raucous contrast to the hard reality of living from August to June in a wilderness marked by months of isolation, frigid rivers, and a constant vigil against the dangers of hostile Indians and wildlife.

The citizens of these ephemeral mountain trading centers represented the entire spectrum of the hunting fraternity: American brigade trappers working under the command of specific companies; Mexicans up from the southern reaches of the Rockies; entire villages of Indians intent on joining the revelry and trading furs, horses, and women for guns and assorted curiosities; French-Canadians and half-breeds, some refugees from the poor wages of the Hudson Bay Company; and the remarkable independent free trappers.

With the arrival of the trade caravans in early July, the trappers began the disposal of furs that represented a year of arduous and often dangerous labor. Prime beaver was worth up to four dollars a pound in the mountains, with an adult pelt weighing in at roughly a pound and a half. The dollar value of the pelts was largely academic, because the trapper was paying outrageously inflated prices for supply goods. As a general rule, what cost the trader one dollar in St. Louis, cost at least ten dollars in the mountains. The necessities of life came high: blankets at $20 apiece, lead at $1 per pound, powder at $4 per pound, knives and hatchets between $3 and $6 each, traps at over $20 apiece, and good Hawken rifles at prices approaching $100. And trade goods such as calico and beads that were used to appease the Indians, could be marked up twenty times.

Even at these rates, acquiring what a mountain man needed seldom consumed even half his pelt pack, and it was then that the trader played his trump card—booze. Alcohol was the fuel that ignited rendezvous and generated the brawling, swaggering, uninhibited behavior that made the event unforgettable. What passed for an alcoholic beverage in the mountains was nothing more than pure grain alcohol purchased in St. Louis, cut four or five times with branch water at the rendezvous site, with a little tobacco thrown in for color and flavor. It did, however, have two redeeming qualities: it made a great deal of money for the traders (whiskey bought in St. Louis for thirty cents a gallon sold at rendezvous for three dollars a pint); and it got the mountain men incredibly drunk in very short order.

The trappers fought, caroused, gambled, and lavished their squaw with high-priced gewgaws. Rough-hewn practical jokes were devised, as when revelers doused a stuporous comrade with alcohol, touched a match to him, and then howled with delight as he whirled like a flaming dervish through camp. Shootings erupted, bones were broken, and the year's wages were often gambled or frittered away in a few days.

They regaled one another with tales of the past year's exploits, describing the new country they had seen, comparing notes on the ever-changing dispositions of Indians they had encountered, and toasting the untimely death of old acquaintances. It was at the rendezvous that any newcomer would be told of such adventures as John Colter's famed 1808 escape from the fierce Blackfoot, a two-hundred-mile, seven-day race for his life over rocky, prickly-pear-covered ground that left the stark-naked Colter full of festering sores and flayed feet by the time he reached Lisa's Fort on the Bighorn River. Or tales of exploration such as Jedediah Smith's two ill-fated treks to California (1826 and 1828), which saw twenty-six out of thirty-three men perish, or Joseph Walker's remarkable 1833 journey to the Pacific in which all fifty-eight men lived to see the next rendezvous.

When the stories were all told, the pelts all traded, and the liquor swilled to the last drop, a mountain man often sobered up to find that he had gambled away horse, rifle, traps, and supplies for the coming year: a circumstance that the traders were only too happy to rectify. A quick conference, a pledge of the next year's catch, and the trapper was outfitted and on his way back to the cold streams and lonely mountains that were his livelihood and life.

One hundred and fifty years later, interest in the lifestyle of the mountain man has undergone a revival, if only in terms of weekend gatherings that simulate rendezvous. Organized competitions such as shoot-outs, knife- and tomahawk-throwing, and archery, have substituted for the wild unpredictability of the old-time debauchery. But, with as many as thirty rendezvous a year recreated in Colorado alone, and an estimated quarter of a million participants nationwide, who dress up as trappers, traders, and their female companions, the rendezvous keeps its grip on America's imagination.

Based on numerous sources, including Donald G. Pike, "World of the Mountain Man," *The American West* 12 (September 1975): 28-35.

Alfred Jacob Miller
Rendezvous Near Green River. c. 1839
Oil on canvas
26 x 38 in
American Heritage Center, University of Wyoming.

55

Alfred Jacob Miller
Presents to Indians. **1858-60**
Watercolor heightened with white on paper
11¼ x 9⁷⁄₁₆ in
The Walters Art Gallery, Baltimore, Maryland.

56

Alfred Jacob Miller
Trapping Beaver. 1858-60
Watercolor on paper
8⅞ x 13¾ in
The Walters Art Gallery, Baltimore, Maryland.

Alfred Jacob Miller
Cavalcade. 1858-60
Watercolor on paper
10⅞ x 15 in
The Walters Art Gallery, Baltimore, Maryland.

John Mix Stanley
Chain of Spires Along the Gila River.
1855
Oil on canvas
31 x 42 in
Phoenix Art Museum;
museum purchase with funds provided by the
Estate of Carolyn Smurthwaite.

In comparing the expedition lithograph with the painting, we see how the artist embellished earlier sketchbook notations to produce his finished work. As expedition artist to General Stephen Watts Kearny's Army of the West in 1846, John Mix Stanley's duty was simply to document what he saw. Nine years later in his Washington, D.C., studio, Stanley painted the fanciful *Chain of Spires Along the Gila River,* 1855, which was more acceptable to the romantic temperament of the time. As Phoenix Art Museum Director James Ballinger points out, it is almost the identical span of years that Henry David Thoreau utilized for *Walden.* Thoreau first moved to the tranquil pond in 1846 and finally published his famous book in 1854.

The site of this painting is in the Mojave Desert between Bitter Spring and Resting Spring. Lieutenant George Brewerton may have painted this scene during his travels over the old Spanish Trail with explorer and adventurer Kit Carson.

George D. Brewerton
Jornada del Muerto. **1853**
Oil on canvas
30 x 44 in
The Oakland Museum, Kahn Collection.
Photo by M. Lee Fatherree.

E. Weber and Company, Lithographers
(after John Mix Stanley)
Chain of Natural Spires Along
the Gila. **1848**
Lithograph
12 x 15 in
Private Collection.

Albert Bierstadt
Merced River, Yosemite Valley. **1866**
Oil on canvas
36 x 50 in
The Metropolitan Museum of Art, Gift of the sons of
William Paton, 1909.

Albert Bierstadt and Fitz Hugh Ludlow, 1863

The notes for the text begin on page 185.

61

The major paintings of Albert Bierstadt (1830-1902) are studio works that generally combine the information from various field sketches and photographs to create an overall composite vision of an "eternal West." As such, the artist's many travels were crucial in providing the details these works are based on. His first trip West in 1859 took him as far as the Wind River Mountains in Wyoming, and shifted the artist's focus on landscape from the Bernese Alps in Switzerland to the glorious new possibilities of the Rocky Mountains and beyond.

As important as this expedition was in terms of new horizons, his 1863 trip with the young writer Fitz Hugh Ludlow (1836-1870) was arguably the experience that most firmly reinforced the Wagnerian vision that would distinguish Bierstadt as the definitive painter of the American West. To say that the artist had an expansive, romantic nature is to understate the obvious, and his friendship with Ludlow proves the point. Ludlow was one of the most celebrated personalities of the day: his book *The Hasheesh Eater* was a bestseller, based on his own experiences, and his chemical-enhanced literary imagination was the rare match for Bierstadt's own vision. Ludlow was given to seeing a battlefield filled with Tartar warriors in a simple pasture, or the full glory of the Nile expanding from the banks of a tiny creek. The fashionably bohemian author cut a colorful figure in New York society, with his beautiful young wife Rosalie at his side. Despite the Civil War, there was a thriving social scene, and they were among the many prominent citizens who frequented the numerous exhibitions and receptions at the famous 10th Street studio, where Bierstadt and so many other artists worked. A close and curious friendship developed between Bierstadt, "the acknowledged prince of the mountain regions," the drug-dependent writer, and the charming, pampered Rosalie.[1] This triangle would take a tantalizing turn in 1866, when Rosalie divorced Ludlow and married Bierstadt—a marriage that lasted until her death in 1893.

But in 1863, with Ludlow's health deteriorating in the city, all agreed that he should accompany Bierstadt on his western trip. One can only imagine the conversations between the two as Bierstadt recounted his own earlier adventures. No doubt their plans took on an increased urgency when they visited the New York exhibition of Carleton Watkins's photographs of Yosemite. Just prior to leaving on their nine-month sojourn, Bierstadt completed a number of pictures based on his earlier trip west, including *Platte River, Nebraska*, 1863 and the great *The Rocky Mountains—"Lander's Peak,"* a title that paid homage to the leader of the artist's first trip west, Colonel Frederick West Lander.

The painting's primary mountain is actually Fremont's Peak in the Wind River Mountains. But Bierstadt's pictures were never meant for the limits of factual accounting, and here he conspicuously prepared himself and his companion, Ludlow, for a West that was well-suited for the extravagancies of description they shared.

The duo left New York in April, traveling by rail as far as Atchison, Kansas. They went in grand style as the guests of two railroad company presidents, due primarily to Bierstadt's lifelong ability to ingratiate himself with influential people. The railroad, of course, was not blind to the obvious prospects for promoting the new tourist areas of the West through such illustrious travelers. In fact, Ludlow's voluminous notes first saw print in the *Atlantic Monthly* between August and December 1864, and eventually became his book, *The Heart of the Continent*. Published in 1871, with illustrations by Bierstadt, it is an effusive account of their journey, written with an urbane flair, for a distinctly eastern audience.

Atchison was the end of the rail line, and stepping out of the luxurious train compartment must have come as a jolt. While awaiting the overland stage that would take them on to Denver and then California, a public hanging took place, drawing a ragtag crowd of some two thousand men, women, and children. In *The Heart of the Continent*, Ludlow describes a dinner that followed where "Women in the dress of ladies leaned across the tea-table and asked, 'Have you been to the hanging?' with as much sang-froid as a New Yorker might say, 'Have you seen Faust?'"[2]

Ludlow had a great instinct for narrative detail, and he would compose his notes into the finished book with the same showmanship Bierstadt would take in orchestrating his sketches into grand canvases. They set out across the prairie at a bumpy pace of one-hundred miles per twenty-four hours aboard a stage driven by a gabbling, profane man who had no fingers on one hand, and who regularly drank himself into oblivion in the driver's box. Ludlow reported the almost comic peril of the stage ride and played it off against the equally breathtaking springtime plenitude of the Great Plains. Both Bierstadt and Ludlow had enough knowledge of plant and animal life to portray the grandeur of landscape with convincing detail, and the author waxes long and poetic about the vast grasslands that then ranged over millions upon millions of acres, full of birds and wild flowers, and dotted with pronghorn antelope.

They would stop over at George Comstock's ranch on the Little Blue River for the purpose of hunting buffalo, one of the *de rigueur* activities of Easterners come West, though Bierstadt would forego the hunt in favor of pictorial opportunities. At first sighting, Ludlow's mind would reel in a chain of his own distinctly urban associations in a fever of enthusiasm: "It was such a strange jumble of feelings to remember operas, National Academy pictures, and the crowd on Broadway, so close on the heels of these grand old giants, who own the monarchy of the continent's freest wilderness."[3] He would go on to describe a wounded buffalo: "From both nostrils the blood was flowing, mixed with glare and foam. His breath was like a blacksmith's bellows. His great sides heaved laboriously, as though he were breathing with his whole body."[4] Bierstadt would hold these scenes in his memory for another twenty-five years before committing the drama to canvas in his late career masterpiece, *The Last of the Buffalo,* 1888.

The awesome power of nature continues to fill Ludlow's text, and his three-page description of a lightning storm over Nebraska is the literary equivalent of Bierstadt's boldest works. Ludlow concludes by saying, "If it were only possible to paint such things! But on canvas they would seem even more theatrical than they do in these inadequate words."[5] While in Denver, they took side trips into the Rockies, and among the many sketches Bierstadt made were studies for *A Storm in the Rockies — Mt. Rosalie,* 1866, the work that most movingly answers the challenge of Ludlow's lightning storm. In the process he named a mountain peak as well as the painting for the present Mrs. Ludlow and future Mrs. Bierstadt.

From Denver they traveled to Salt Lake City, and on to California across the vast Utah-Nevada desert, still by stage, still in the rapture of an adventure that could offer its share of unexpected surprises. Indeed, they encountered the smoldering ruins of an Indian attack on an overland station, the smell of the roasting flesh of its six murdered inhabitants still in the air, and thus became alerted to a whole new series of possibilities in the landscape.

It was with a sense of great relief that they arrived in San Francisco on July 17, 1863, and checked into the elegant Occidental Hotel. Within a few days they were on their way into the Sierras and the promised visit to Yosemite. Thomas Ayers had been the first artist to sketch the valley in 1855, and by 1863 it was a popular, if remote, scenic attraction. Bierstadt would soon make this place his own personal territory of the mind with works that took Ludlow's description of the view from Inspiration Point as a given: "We did not so much seem to be seeing from that crag of vision a new scene on the old familiar globe as a new heaven and a new earth into which the creative spirit had just been breathed."[6]

After seven weeks' camp, and daily sketching "in their divine workshop,"[7] they would travel north to Oregon and on a crisp autumn day in the Willamette Valley witness seven snow-capped peaks of the Cascades in one sighting. But it would be the Rockies and most especially the Sierras that would prove the lasting sources of inspiration from an adventure of "half a score of white men all alone in the heart of the virgin continent."[8]

Four months after their return to New York, the 1864 Metropolitan Fair in aid of the Sanitary Commission assured Bierstadt's artistic preeminence. There — among six hundred other paintings — the huge painting that acted as a beacon for the recent trip, *The Rocky Mountains — "Lander's Peak,"* 1863, held its own with Frederick Church's masterwork, *The Heart of the Andes,* 1859. The two canvases faced each other in the exhibition, in a dramatic duel between two of America's greatest painters. Bierstadt's was the popular favorite, likely due to the nationalistic subject matter, enhanced by the connection to Lander who had recently died in the Civil War. The painting would sell for $25,000 the following year, the most ever for an American artwork. Furthermore, the artist had engravings made by master engraver James Smillie, offered in three limited editions, for a net of $23,500.[9] In 1866, the year Bierstadt and Rosalie were married, *A Storm in the Rockies — Mt. Rosalie* was heralded as an even greater success. The importance of the trip with Ludlow would be underscored again that year as Bierstadt began his first paintings of Yosemite, such as *Merced River, Yosemite Valley,* 1866.

Albert Bierstadt
The Rocky Mountains. c. 1863
Chromolithograph
21⅜ x 34½ in
Amon Carter Museum, Fort Worth.

Thomas A. Ayres
*General View of the Great
Yo-semite Valley, Mariposa County,
California. 1859*
Toned lithograph (handcolored)
13¾ x 21⁵⁄₁₆ in
Amon Carter Museum, Fort Worth.

In 1855, Thomas Ayers became the first artist to sketch Yosemite. His initial visit came at the invitation of James Mason Hutchings, a journalist from San Francisco who used the spectacular views of Yosemite to launch his publishing venture, the *California Illustrated* magazine.

Though these works had their detractors for being melodramatic, they also inspired critics to claim the paintings could "illumine a twilight room," and portray places where "into the very vestibule of virgin Nature…The King of the World…stands dwarfed in the valley, mutely, hopelessly gazing whither Nature is closeted alone with God!"[10] Such lavish responses read like any number of Ludlow's own descriptions of western landscape: "The slabs [of rock] might have been hot tiles on the roof of some impenetrable Dantesque hell; the buttresses waited for another story of the prison which should build itself to heaven."[11] These were clearly two kindred spirits who complemented each other's unrestrained visions of what the art of the West could convey. The next few years continued to be great ones for Bierstadt, but a downward spiral set in for Ludlow, who remained troubled with drugs and bad health, and who died in Switzerland in 1870.

Bierstadt's years of triumph would also fade, and *The Last of the Buffalo,* 1888 would serve as a final, poignant footnote to the 1863 trip, for it was rejected by the American committee for inclusion in the Paris Exposition of 1889. Considered by the fifty-eight-year-old artist as one of his finest, it was in style, scale, and subject, simply out of fashion with the more Impressionist sensibility of the time. And yet its wider public response stimulated the first official census of American buffalo, a species which as late as 1850 had numbered some 20 million. By 1889, that number was reduced to a total of 551 head, and the Indian cultures were suffering a parallel fate.

Bierstadt was normally a painter of timeless treasures despite his own specific and various experiences in the West. Thus, *The Last of the Buffalo* is a singular enigma in his oeuvre. If it is not simply an exotic, romantic view of the past with a sentimental title based on his 1863 sketches, what is it? Certainly Bierstadt had enough firsthand experience in the West to know Indian people were not responsible for the ultimate destruction of the buffalo. And he had written letters as early as 1859 describing the tragic passing of the Native American's way of life. We can see for certain, however, that the image is remarkable in at least one respect: the "limitless" Bierstadtian landscape is a mere backdrop to the disquieting slaughter on center stage, a rare acknowledgment by this artist of a West that was beginning to discover the limits of the western adventure.

Albert Bierstadt
Platte River, Nebraska. **1863**
Oil on canvas
36 x 57½ in
Manoogian Collection

Albert Bierstadt
The Last of the Buffalo. c. 1888
Oil on canvas
60¼ x 96½ in
Courtesy of the Buffalo Bill Historical Center, Cody, Wyoming.

Albert Bierstadt
Rocky Mountains, "Lander's Peak."
1863
Oil on canvas
44⅜ x 36½ in
Courtesy of The Fogg Art Museum, Harvard
University, Cambridge, Massachusetts, Bequest
of Mrs. William Hayes Fogg.

Albert Bierstadt
Passing Storm Over the Sierra Nevadas. 1870
Oil on canvas
52x71 in

Lent by The San Antonio Museum Association. Purchased with funds provided by the Robert J. Kleberg, Jr., and Helen C. Kleberg Foundation.

Thomas Moran
Grand Canyon of the Yellowstone.
1893
Oil on canvas
19½ x 15½ in
The Fine Arts Museums of San Francisco,
Gift of Mr. and Mrs. John D. Rockefeller 3rd.

Thomas Moran and the Yellowstone, 1870-1872

Thomas Moran's most famous paintings—so important in the formation of the National Park System—are commonly attributed to his first trip to the American Far West in 1871, the year he accompanied Ferdinand V. Hayden's expedition to the Yellowstone. But Moran actually first illustrated such geographic wonders of the Yellowstone as Castle Geyser, Tower Falls, and Grotto Geyser, almost a year before he actually saw the area himself. These were works of the imagination, based on someone else's firsthand information, and were the first widely seen visual evidence of this mysterious place.

In 1805 Lewis and Clark had mapped the Yellowstone River as a primary tributary of the Missouri, but did not follow it to its source, even though they had heard tales from the Indians of a strange place possessed of spirits. But one of their party, John Colter, returned to the mountains at the end of the expedition. During a solitary journey in 1807, Colter found the area that would become Yellowstone National Park. His descriptions of boiling springs, volcanic activity, and the smell of brimstone soon caused the place to be known as "Colter's Hell."

Not until 1827 was anything recorded in print of the wonders of the Yellowstone, and it continued to be regarded as a place existing somewhere between fact and fiction until 1870 when an expedition led by Nathaniel P. Langford traveled there. Langford kept a fully detailed diary of the extraordinary sights he encountered, which would be published in *Scribner's Monthly*. Two of his party made crude sketches of some of the more amazing natural formations, though these pictures were not published and remained relatively obscure documents for over a century.

But in 1980, a rather odd group of black-and-white paintings carrying Thomas Moran's signature were purchased by a private collector on the supposition that they were early works by the famous painter of the West, perhaps done after the photographs of William Henry Jackson in 1871. The staff of the Gilcrease Institute in Tulsa, Oklahoma, was contacted in an effort to verify the supposition, and during the course of research something quite different was discovered. Distinct similarities were noted between these paintings of Moran's and his wood engravings that appeared in the May and June 1871 issues of *Scribner's Monthly*.

Further similarities were found to exist in crude sketches by Walter Trumbull and Charles Moore of the 1870 Langford expedition, which was the basis of the *Scribner's* article. Continued research by the staff and subsequent authentication confirmed the speculation that Moran's first pictures of the Yellowstone were indeed based on the sketches by Trumbull and Moore, painted almost a year before Moran ever crossed the Mississippi, on an assignment for *Scribner's*.

It turned out that Langford provided the newly formed magazine with his article on the 1870 expedition along with his companions' primitive drawings. However, the editors of *Scribner's*, in an effort to compete with *Harper's Magazine*, wanted to illustrate the issues with high quality, believable, wood engravings, and the sketches by Trumbull and Moore were simply too crude to be used. Fortunately for everyone involved, Philadelphia artist Thomas Moran had been working for *Scribner's Monthly*. Aided by Langford's descriptions, Moran reworked the amateurs' sketches into a series of fourteen black-and-white wash paintings from which wood engravings were made.

After the *Scribner's Monthly* project was completed, Moran, fascinated by the area, found a way to see the Yellowstone firsthand in the summer of 1871, this time as a member of the Hayden survey party. The superb sketches Moran made proved to be important supporting documents for Hayden's report and along with William Henry Jackson's photographs, were instrumental in convincing the government to make the Yellowstone the first national park in 1872. They also formed the groundwork on which Moran built a lifelong career of painting definitive scenes of the most spectacular landscapes of the West.

This material is adapted from Anne Morand, "Introduction," *The Art of the Yellowstone 1870-1872* (Tulsa, Oklahoma: Thomas Gilcrease Museum Association, 1983), 4-15. Reprinted with permission from Anne Morand.

SCRIBNER'S MONTHLY.

VOL. II.   MAY, 1871.   No. 1.

I HAD indulged, for several years, a great curiosity to see the wonders of the upper valley of the Yellowstone. The stories told by trappers and mountaineers of the natural phenomena of that region were so strange and marvelous that, as long ago as 1866, I first contemplated the possibility of organizing an expedition for the express purpose of exploring it. During the past year, VOL. II.—1

meeting with several gentlemen who expressed like curiosity, we determined to make the journey in the months of August and September.

The Yellowstone and Columbia, the first flowing into the Missouri and the last into the Pacific, divided from each other by the Rocky Mountains, have their sources within a few miles of each other. Both rise in the mountains which separate Idaho from the new Territory of Wyoming, but the headwaters of the Yellowstone are only accessible from Montana. The mountains surrounding the basin from which they flow are very lofty, covered with pines, and on the southeastern side present to the traveler a precipitous wall of rock, several thousand feet in height. This barrier prevented Captain Reynolds from visiting the headwaters of the Yellowstone while prosecuting an expedition planned by the Government and placed under his command, for the purpose of exploring that river, in 1859.

The source of the Yellowstone is in a

Thomas Moran
The Castle Geyser, Upper Geyser Basin,
Yellowstone National Park. **1874**
Chromolithograph
8¼ x 12½ in
Amon Carter Museum, Fort Worth.

71

Thomas Moran
Hot Springs of Gardiner's River,
Yellowstone National Park. **1875**
Chromolithograph
8¼ x 12½ in
Amon Carter Museum, Fort Worth.

Thomas Moran
The Great Hot Spring,
Gardiner's River. **1872**
Watercolor on paper
9 x 13¼ in
The Thomas Gilcrease Institute of American History
and Art, Tulsa, Oklahoma.

72

Thomas Moran
Tower Falls. 1872
Watercolor on paper
11¼ x 7¾ in
The Thomas Gilcrease Institute of American History
and Art, Tulsa, Oklahoma.

Private Charles Moore
Tower Falls. 1870
Pencil on paper
7 7/16 x 9 1/8 in
National Park Service

Thomas Moran
Tower Falls, Tower Creek, Wyoming.
1870
Black and white wash on paper
8 1/2 x 5 in
The Thomas Gilcrease Institute of American History
and Art, Tulsa, Oklahoma.

Thomas Moran
Tower Falls.
Scribner's Monthly, May, 1871
University of Washington Libraries.

Walter Trumbull
Castle Geyser Cone. **1870**
Pencil on paper
4 x 7¹¹⁄₁₆ in
National Park Service.

Thomas Moran
The Castle Geyser, Montana. **1870**
Black and white wash on paper
4¾ x 8⅛ in
The Thomas Gilcrease Institute of American History
and Art, Tulsa, Oklahoma.

Thomas Moran
Crater of the Castle Geyser.
Scribner's Monthly, **May, 1871**
University of Washington Libraries.

Thomas Moran
Grand Canyon of the Arizona. **1902**
Oil on canvas
14 x 20 in
Private Collection. Photo by Richard Nichol.

Thomas Moran first came to the Grand Canyon in 1873 as the guest of John Wesley Powell, who led the first descent of the Colorado River in 1869. Moran confessed his artistic skills inadequate when faced with the challenge of the Grand Canyon, and yet he returned here repeatedly over the next forty-seven years to sketch and photograph in preparation for his finished paintings.

Thomas Moran
Cliffs of Green River. **1874**
Oil on canvas
25⅛ x 45⅜ in
Amon Carter Museum, Fort Worth.

Thomas Moran saw these towering buttes when he disem-
barked from the train that brought him west for the first time
in 1871. This area near Toll-Gate Rock, on the Green River in
Wyoming, had once been a location of the mountain men's
annual rendezvous and was later the site of Captain Bonne-
ville's first fort. It was also the starting point of John Wesley
Powell's descent of the Colorado River to the Grand Canyon.
There has been conjecture that the figures in the painting
represent Powell's expedition since this painting is thought
to have been owned by him.

William Bell
Grand Canyon of the Colorado River,
Mouth of Kanab Wash, Looking East.
1872
Albumen print
10¾ x 7⅞ in
Collection of Mark Klett.

A View of the Grand Canyon in Homage to William Bell

Mark Klett

"Things aren't what they used to be; and what's worse, they never were."[1]

John Szarkowski

William Henry Jackson
Expedition of 1870. **1870**
Albumen print
5⅝ x 7¾ in
The Denver Public Library,
Western History Department.

The notes for the text begin on page 186.

On a bright summer afternoon I stood upon the precipice of the Grand Canyon overlooking a scene made familiar by a photograph taken more than one hundred years ago. Sixty miles of gravel road, several more miles of jeep track, and a half-mile hike brought me to the exact spot where, in 1872, William Bell photographed the canyon from its north rim. As the Colorado River descended to the west, I could study its banks while holding a copy of his picture.

I had traveled to this spot to pursue my own expedition of a sort. I wanted to rediscover, as best one can today, what is perhaps our most monumental and sacred western landscape. It is a place for which the traveler's expectations are groomed by a long history of photographs describing the canyon's vantage points, vistas, rock formations, light, and color in every season. I wondered if there was anything new I could add to a subject that must already contribute significantly to Eastman Kodak's film sales. Rather than shun them, I decided to embrace photographs from the past as a way of comparing my own, contemporary, experience of the canyon. Bell's picture was among the earliest made there, and I wondered what, if anything, I could learn about this landscape from his photograph.

Bell's photograph was made for Lieutenant George Wheeler's Geological and Geographical Survey of the 100th Meridian (1871-1879) where it was included, along with other photographs and lithographs, in a report of the party's field territory. Other now well-known photographers, including Timothy O'Sullivan, William Henry Jackson, and John K. Hillers, were similarly employed by the western surveys of the 1860s and 1870s. Teams directed by Ferdinand V. Hayden, John Wesley Powell, and Clarence King typically included natural scientists, topographers, anthropologists, military engineers, and, occasionally, artists. It has long been thought that photographers traveled with these expeditions to make illustrations of scientific interest. In practice, their photographs were probably more useful as general descriptions of the landscapes covered by survey parties than as topographical documents. Landscape views verified the geographical expanse of the survey's accomplishments, and in this important respect helped sell Congress on continued appropriations. In spite of their utilitarian duties, the survey photographers have, in recent years, been elevated to the stature of fine artists. Their prints have acquired value as aesthetic as well as historical artifacts. Whether or not one agrees with the shift of focus onto the image-makers instead of historical contexts for their work, the impact of these survey photographers' images on how we view the West has demanded, and is receiving, much analysis.

Bell's picture had long been a favorite of mine. On the left-hand side of the view, a round, head-shaped rock suggests a sign of human presence. Yet standing at Bell's vantage point, I was surprised to find that the rock was not round at all, but a rectangular slab of sandstone with a curved edge tilting precariously toward the canyon's rim. Bell had simply used the slab to provide a strong graphic frame for the scene. The head shape was created by his cropping and choice of where to place his camera. And here I found that Bell was something of a daredevil, since in order to create this perspective his camera was set virtually at the brink of the precipice, an almost vertical drop of one-half mile.

In the distance of Bell's photograph the canyon reflected the last strong light before sunset, when the sun was low and shadows were cast from one wall to the next. As I waited for the time of day to approximate when Bell took his picture, I noticed that my shadow dominated the view's foreground. Bell's own shadow must have been a part of what he witnessed at the site, too, though he skillfully avoided including it in the picture. From a subtle dark tone in the lower left corner of the photograph, there is evidence his shadow was there and framed out of the composition.

I wondered at the relationship between Bell's creation of the head-rock and the unavoidable sign of one's presence at the scene. Whether or not Bell paid it much notice, this self-consciousness interested me. As I became aware of the practical decisions he made in order to photograph the canyon, I became more sensitive to my own experience at the site, and understood how my perspective is derived, in part, from 19th-century sensibilities.

Standing where Bell once stood I felt a mixture of surprise along with success in tracking down his image. I had studied his picture carefully in the weeks before leaving home, but I was still unprepared for the immensity of the vistas and for the apparent lack of change in the canyon before me. It became possible to envision time existing on another, grander scale: one for which a century was hardly an instant. Though Bell's picture was the product of an era completely different from my own, we seemed to share a physical space that had yet to be altered by an incomprehensible order of tectonic forces. The rocks and ledges were nearly identical; in fact, from visual comparisons alone it was almost possible for me to imagine, if only for a moment, that Bell's photograph was made a week and not a century before my arrival.

But at the same moment the illusion was shattered. On the river, twenty-seven hundred feet below, tiny rubber rafts appeared and then disappeared in the midst of distant rapids. Two kayaks passed through the fastest water with them. Their occupants then paddled to shore, walked upriver with their boats, and ran the rapids again. I remember reading the journals of John Wesley Powell, the first to navigate the Grand Canyon only a few years before Bell made his photograph. Powell's experience was remarkably different, and he would have been aghast at repeating rapids for sport. He was concerned his party might not survive their journey, and upon reaching open spaces at the end of the canyon's white water wrote: "The first hour of convalescent freedom seems rich recompense for all the pain and gloom and terror."[2] To Powell, the Grand Canyon was a prison.

From the safe perspective of another century these terrors seem romantic. Those of us who seek wilderness savor the threat of the river's power, as long as we have brought the right equipment. We relive Powell's wilderness adventure, and it is still a challenge in spite of the Glen Canyon Dam far out of view. The dam, built in 1963, put an end to this stretch of river wildness, but once on the water it is easy to forget that the flow rate can be controlled with the technological authority of a giant washroom faucet. Where the dam crosses the river, a daily train of recreational vehicles passes with names like *Travel-Eze, Wanderer, Road Ranger, Idle-Time,* and *Me-Too.*

As I contemplated the picture and the scene it represents, I knew that important changes had occurred. Like the rafters below, the evidence is subtle, hardly more than tiny details in this photographic panorama. Yet, an earlier experience taught me that the subtlest details are often the most revealing.

Past experience gave me the idea to search for the exact site of Bell's picture. Between 1977 and 1979 I helped rephotograph more than 120 19th-century expedition photographs for the Rephotographic Survey Project (RSP). The RSP, funded by the National Endowment for the Arts and the Polaroid Corporation, experimented with photography's ability to address time, space, and myth on a scale only the vastness of the American West and the time space of a century could supply.

The RSP was a collaborative effort reflecting the motivations of five participants. We were concerned with changes in the western landscape, with historical information about 19th-century photographers, and with the concept of comparing two similar but different images. We became especially interested in how survey photographs, as artifacts of a moment, have come to represent (or misrepresent) a place with historical authority.

Timothy O'Sullivan
Historic Spanish Record of the Conquest. 1873
Albumen print
20x24 in
Collection of Gus Kayafas

Linda Connor
Spanish Alphabet, Inscription Rock, New Mexico. 1983
Silver print
8x10 in
Courtesy Etherton/Stern Gallery, Tucson, Arizona.

81

The project had a precise methodology that attempted to duplicate the vantage point, lighting, and other physical conditions of an original image. The resulting photo pairs showed some of the major physical changes that have occurred in the western landscape, but they did so without explaining the causes of these changes, or providing the contexts in which they occurred. Many sites the RSP rephotographed were much like Bell's view of the Grand Canyon, in that there was little or no change between pictures. What the rephotographs could not show was sometimes to be found outside the picture frame, information that was often contradictory to what the combined photo pair implied. For example, in rephotographing William Henry Jackson's *Whitehouse Mountain and Elk Lake,* 1873 (areas now called Snowmass Mountain and Geneva Lake), we found that the wilderness area showed virtually no difference when the view was limited to the confines of Jackson's photograph. Just outside of our rephotograph's borders, however, were campers staked out in brightly colored tents, listening to portable stereos and drinking beer (one should also wonder what was at the edges of Jackson's picture). By themselves each photo pair, an original photograph with a simple but precise rephotograph, was unable to provide complete information about the scenes they were recording. Nor were they meant to.

The RSP * taught us that while two pictures together may illustrate change, they cannot explain the more complex history of our connection to the land. They can tell us only about what is in one picture and not the other; but that is often enough to raise questions we might never have thought to ask.

*For further information on the Survey Photographers, see page 90.

When Timothy O'Sullivan traveled through Nevada with Clarence King's U.S. Geological Exploration of the Fortieth Parallel, in 1868 (four years before Bell's Grand Canyon trek), he hauled his equipment in a special horse-drawn wagon. One of his more famous images shows this wagon standing below some unnamed Nevada sand dunes. It is a wonderfully composed image, and easy to saddle with nostalgia, but it never occurred to me before the RSP that O'Sullivan's movements were restricted to where that wagon could travel and how far he could run from it while carrying a drying, collodion-covered glass plate. (Considering the process, it isn't surprising that we found most pioneer photographers' pictures were made close to a 19th-century road.)

At the canyon, after paying homage to Bell's picture, I moved a few miles to the end of the dirt road at Toroweap Point. Toroweap is one of the few places along the canyon's western extension that is accessible by automobile. The view there is stunning and also the subject of two other 19th-century photographs. I discovered that John K. Hillers visited the point for the Powell survey sometime after 1872. One of his images is aimed upriver, the other downriver. Though I had seen both photographs before this trip, I never suspected the two were made only a few hundred yards apart.

Besides the vista, what really caught my attention at Toroweap was a logbook kept in a covered box near the rim's edge and close to Hillers's vantage points. The log is a loosely bound notebook, a kind of public record placed at the site by the National Park Service for the purpose (I could only assume) of recording the numbers of visitors and the length of their stay, while also giving them a small space for commentary. The comments made fascinating reading. I entered my name in the log and was startled by the following plea written several months earlier:

Ranger or Anyone we are in the lower campground (1st spur road to right). Broken down. NEED HELP.

Next to this was the reply: *Go to Hell!*

And below that another: *We need beer!*

At first this seemed like a prank, but reading further it was clear this log was a record of the pleasures, expectations, sense of humor (or lack of), and oftentimes disappointments, of late 20th-century western travelers:

What happened to the quiet and beautiful solitude that once was here? Written alongside: *Why don't you help by staying away?*

This place is still unspoiled and it makes me think clearly and almost gives me an orgasm.

Blow up the Glen Canyon Dam; eliminate the aircraft, keep out the cigarette smokers and this would be as lovely as it was 100 or 1000 or 10,000 years ago. (PS— the [picnic] tables can stay, but take it off all the maps and don't mark the road. If you love it— leave it alone!!)

We drive two days to find peace and some guy asks us if he can hang his hammock at our camp! Go back to your computer convention.
You need to fix this place up to get some real crowds in here. Put up a billboard on 389 at the turnoff and pave the road. If you do this you can probably get some use out of this place. You also need to put up guard rails to make it safe. If you cut down the vegetation, there will be less fire danger. It would also be a good idea to pick up all the rocks. Sooner or later someone's going to trip and fall. All the people in the condos won't like to see dozens of airplanes all day. You should make the air taxi people use 747s. That way there would be one plane every hour. If you got enough people to come here, it would pay to put an elevator down to the river. You could build McDonalds in the canyon. Just think how great it would be. You really need to build this place up if it's going to be of any use.

Below this response:
Its use, sir, might be to make oneself HUMBLE, period!
The encroachment of civilization will wreck this place if not controlled now!!

(And I thought: is it already too late?)

Timothy O'Sullivan
Sand Dunes, Carson Desert, Nevada.
1868
Albumen print
7⅞ x 10¾ in
Collection of the U.S. Geological Survey.

• Carleton Watkins
Dam and Lake, Nevada County. **1871**
Albumen print
The J. Paul Getty Museum.

The logbook indicated that people came to Toroweap to throw off contemporary life; and, in a real sense, to remove themselves from our time. Unfortunately, reminders of what they left behind seem unavoidable, like the airplane sight-seeing tours passing overhead. As I traveled along the canyon I almost understood the sentiments of several Toroweap log entries wishing for a 20mm cannon to shoot these planes down. While upriver at Point Sublime, sixteen annoying, low-flying aircraft buzzed past in only one hour.

The logbook reminded me that people seeking wilderness have often wanted to escape not only from one another but from rules that confine their behavior. Over a century ago some sought to escape the restrictions of governance by moving farther away from settlements. And it may not be coincidence that modern-day explorers often seek to escape the bureaucracies of landscape management. Of the illusions that history has emphasized about the land, perhaps the most powerful is the one that tells us that our return to wilderness ennobles us, gives us rebirth. In this respect, the well-worn hero myths of Western movies and pulp serials play out an often repeated morality story that bears comparing to the photographs we have inherited. In these tales, the settlement of the frontier can be seen as a struggle by individuals of strong character to end threats faced in conquering savage territories. Even today this is the preferred story of winning the West: a conversion by strength of wilderness from threat to subservience.

In reality the forces at work in the 19th century were far different from individuals wrestling with clear moral choices, fighting noble, often solitary battles to control their destinies. The photographs from the 19th century actually indicate that the period involved a wholesale exploitation of the landscape. Many photographs contain the ruthless evidence of clear-cutting, hydraulic mining, and road building. Today these images are often overlooked in favor of the more romantic among them, and the exploration photographers are characterized as recorders of a wilderness lost. This is a generalization that preordains visions of a ruined contemporary landscape.

For their part, the 19th-century photographers made small, but important contributions to the winning of the West by investing in the landscape a vision that coincided with an expanding nationalistic agenda. The photographers helped to name, open, and otherwise assume ownership of what was previously inaccessible, and in doing so became as important a part of their time as the spectacular landscapes being recorded. It was a first step toward gaining control over a place soon to

Eliot Porter
Clouds at Sunset, Tesuque, New Mexico, July, 1959.
Photograph-dye transfer print
8½ x 8¼ in
Courtesy of Scheinbaum and Russek, Santa Fe, New Mexico.

become home to thousands of Americans. That helps explain why in Powell's day the signs of advancing civilization were prized as achievements, not spurned as exploitation, and why tree stumps made good foregrounds for those photographing growing 19th-century townships.

As an example consider what was perhaps the 19th century's most influential, and egocentric, American landscape photograph, William Henry Jackson's *Mountain of the Holy Cross, Great National Range, Colorado,* 1873. The photograph with its cross of snow atop one of the central Rocky Mountains' highest peaks became an instant success with East Coast viewers who were seeing the western landscape recorded for the first time. It fit the popular view of a Manifest Destiny (i.e., God gave us this land to achieve greatness), and the image was made publicly accessible by virtue of the medium's repeatability. Jackson hastened to reap the artistic and financial benefits of his photograph. Later, tales of the cross discovery were embellished, and other parts of the photograph were identified to create a religious tableau from the scene. In producing copies of the photograph, Jackson even retouched the negative by adding a waterfall below the patch of snow next to the cross. The snow patch was nicknamed the "Snow Angel." The angel's arms were outstretched in prayer, and its tears of mourning ran below to the waterfall and filled a small lake called "The Bowl of Tears." At last a myth had been documented with the camera's veracity, and it may be as close as any 19th-century photographer ever came to filling a hero's mold.

The belief that wilderness offers unlimited material and spiritual wealth has since been devalued, and looking at the 19th-century pictures helped me to understand how far contemporary views have shifted from those of our explorer predecessors. With increasing population and limited resources it is easy to feel a loss in our connection with the land. On top of that, the destructive powers of our technologies concern us more than any natural threats long ago brought under submission. In an interesting (but also egocentric) reversal, wilderness is now seen as the place that can save us from ourselves. Whereas in the 19th century we wielded divine power at the top of a natural order, in the 20th century we are sinners in need of atonement, and must be cast out of the garden because we have spoiled it. Today the land is thought beautiful only when man is absent. This is evident in the comments at Toroweap, but in a more official capacity it also guides our government's wilderness policy. The Wilderness Act of 1964 contains this definition of wilderness: "A wilderness, in contrast with those areas where man and his own works dominate the landscape, is hereby recognized as an area where the earth and its community of life are untrammeled by man, where man himself is a visitor who does not remain."[3] There is irony in this design. We may be protecting the land from our further material exploits, but in a most important respect we continue to see ourselves as outsiders to paradise. We are still separated from the landscape we love.

From the practical experience of the survey photographers it would have been hard to imagine a time when fear of loosing the wilderness would spawn the Sierra Club, The Wilderness Society, and Greenpeace to name a few. In the 1870s the lands seemed so vast, so remote, travel was so slow. And unlike photographers on the East Coast, where the landscape had been interpreted long before the invention of photography, western cameramen/explorers were able to choose first-time subjects, and their selections set precedents. The 19th-century photographers underscored a sense of the monumental in the western landscape, and that has had a lasting effect on how the West is seen to this day. Many of their pictorial devices, the framing of space, scale, and use of unusual vantage points, are still used by 20th-century land-scapists. The camera continues to be a device for exploration, and the "photographic journey," the modern descendant of the geographical survey, has become laden with its own myths and heroes. For some photographers this journey has become a search to find idealized 19th-century landscapes. The difference, however, is that the concern has shifted from the discovery of wilderness places to their preservation. The underlying theme affirms the beauty and value of the natural world amidst its declining availability.

The long history of photography's role in landscape pres-ervation began, appropriately enough, with William Henry Jackson's pic-tures of Yellowstone, which were used to influence Congress in favor of creating the first national park in 1872. In this century, photographers working in cooperation with environmental organizations, have helped sway public opinion in favor of preserving remaining wilderness areas. The Sierra Club, under its former director David Brower, took an early lead in the 1960s, publishing photography books with an environmental emphasis. The color photographs of Elliot Porter, Phillip Hyde, and others instilled an appreciation for the West's natural, timeless, beauty. Since then almost all similarly concerned organizations have followed suit, enlarging the list of publications to include photographic calendars, engagement notebooks, magazines, and assorted posters.

Reading the Toroweap logbook, however, I couldn't help but recall what Colin Fletcher (author of *The Complete Walker*) once said: "The woods are overrun and sons of bitches like me are half the problem."[4] Could contemporary photographs have had deleterious effects because they have popularized places like this? Have they also increased visitor pressure, or created expectations about the purity of what we should and should not find? (For an example of practical pressure consider this: reservations are now required on many national park backcountry trails; and in Yosemite National Park tickets for the campgrounds may be pur-chased in advance from Ticketron outlets.) One could argue these are the inevitable costs of preserving wild lands in a democracy, but on a prac-tical as well as philosophical level, publicizing wilderness areas leads to some unsettling dilemmas for today's environmentally concerned photographers.

The most unsettling feeling I had standing at the canyon's rim, watching the planes above and the rafts below, was that of confusion, the result of comparing my contemporary experiences to a past I had only imagined. Toroweap is not the wilderness I had come to expect from looking at photographs. I had hoped for a place still untouched, but it takes an effort to avoid the traces of human presence: an effort similar to Bell's cropping of his shadow from his photograph. (By the way, this is not an obsolete gesture. I know photographers, otherwise purists, who spot out the jet contrails in their skies.) My experience confronts a few of the myths that photographs have helped to create about this place. This is no longer open territory from which one can count on the free-doms of solitude, or a setting in which one can wrestle control over destiny. Toroweap remains a landscape of impressive scale and beauty, which has not physically vanished with the 19th century, but it has been effectively changed by an increasing number of uses to the point where its status as wilderness has become problematic. I could only wonder, and worry about the part I might play as a contemporary image-maker in determining this landscape's future.

86

Carleton Emmons Watkins
Yosemite Valley from the Best
General View. **c. 1865**
Albumen print
From The American Geographical Society
Collection, University of
Wisconsin-Milwaukee Library.

So as I drove back to where Bell had made his photograph on the north rim, I faced some tough questions. I wanted to make my own picture of the scene, but what might ordinarily be a simple act was suddenly loaded with responsibility: If I show a pristine landscape, do I overlook the growing human presence and invite viewing the canyon as an awaiting frontier? If I show signs of human influence do I accept or criticize them? If I feel disdain for what I see, should I advocate political activism or confirm the importance of what's left and show that our relationship to the land need not be adversarial? I confess it was tempting to recreate Bell's vision rather than deal with the complex issues of the present. Yet it didn't feel possible, or wise, for me to avoid commenting on this landscape as an occupied territory: a place that the culture consciously manages to meet the growing demand for resources, urban expansion, defense, recreation, and more. I felt that re-exploring this place with a camera called for a different approach, one which also re-examines our relationship to wilderness, including the substantial role we play in defining it.

The present challenge lies in making photographs that address our western landscape myths in ways that make sense out of contemporary western experience. As I stood feeling dwarfed by my surroundings, the conceptual aspects of this job suddenly seemed as vast as the landscape. The difficulty, it seems, is to discover new wilderness values as well as new wilderness places. This means cultivating an appreciation for the land based not in spite of the fact that it has been touched by us, but because, in almost every aspect, it has been.

The challenge of these ideas was both exciting and intimidating, and as I settled to the practical task of making a photograph, rather abstract. As so often happens in the field, the most pressing questions are pragmatic. It may be a fine goal to tackle the redefinition of landscape myths, but I was grappling with where to place the camera, what to frame, what lens to use, and when to take my picture. The camera sat on its tripod looking somewhat forlorn as I puzzled over these many questions. It was when I paused to study the scene *around* Bell's view that I noticed that my sunglasses, as well as my shadow, were at the edge of the scene. It was like recognizing O'Sullivan's footprints in his picture of the Nevada sand dunes. My instantaneous reaction was to grab my wide-angle lens and place Bell's view within the context of these two signs of my own presence. Just another egocentric gesture, I thought as I made the exposure.

The picture seemed only to hint at the many ways this place and our attitudes about it have changed in the last century. Nonetheless it felt like an honest response to the earlier vision that had guided me; and more importantly, it convinced me I could do more than observe this place in the same way as my predecessor. I felt free to let go of Bell's vision, to comment on my firsthand experience, and to participate in a still evolving history of the land's visual representation. However small its contribution, that picture was gratifying, and it seemed to make the whole trip worthwhile.

Mark Klett is a photographer and studio manager of the Photography Collaborative Facility at the School of Art at Arizona State University. A recipient of two fellowships from the National Endowment for the Arts, his work has been exhibited nationally and internationally. He organized with JoAnn Verburg the Rephotographic Survey Project in 1985.

Mark Klett
A View of the Grand Canyon in
Homage to William Bell, East of
Toroweap. **1988**
Silver print
16 x 20 in
Courtesy of the Fraenkel Gallery, San Francisco.

The Survey Photographers, 1867-1879

The photographers who documented the West between 1867 and 1879 were affiliated with particular geological surveys led by Clarence King, John Wesley Powell, Lieutenant George Wheeler, or Ferdinand Vandeveer Hayden. These scientific explorers understood the benefits of taking photographers on the surveys, despite their cumbersome equipment. The pictures themselves offered unalterable documentation of the geography and activities of the survey. Photographers either confirmed or put to rest tales spread by earlier western explorers and could impress the public with pictures of incredible geological wonders. Surveyors had various motives in appointing official photographers, but each leader was competing for public recognition and financial support from the United States government.

Before the Civil War, the government had sponsored exploration of former Mexican territories primarily in order to establish travel routes between the East and West coasts. One of the first survey "photographers" was S. N. Carvalho, actually a daguerreotypist, who accompanied Colonel Robert C. Fremont across the Great Divide in 1853. Unfortunately Carvalho's plates were lost. Other early attempts at photo documentation of western exploration proved unsuccessful as well, due to the technical deficiencies of the time.

However, with the outbreak of the Civil War, the famous portrait photographer and New York and Washington, D.C., studio owner Mathew Brady, saw the opportunity for even greater recognition. Photographing the Battle of Bull Run in 1861 only increased his fame, despite the fact that his apprentices did most of the shooting. Any photograph to leave any of his five studios, despite the photographer, was stamped with Brady's name. One of his apprentices, Timothy O'Sullivan, would eventually surpass his teacher in fame and skill. O'Sullivan took numerous pictures of the Civil War for Brady and Alexander Gardner, former manager of Brady's Washington, D.C., studio. Unlike Brady, Gardner believed in acknowledging the photographer. Nearly half of the photographs in Gardner's *Photographic Sketch Book of the Civil War* are credited to O'Sullivan.

Government-sponsored westward explorations resumed after the Civil War. Clarence King created the "United States Geological Exploration of the Fortieth Parallel" in 1867 to survey the region between the Rocky Mountains and Sierra Nevadas. Well-established by his war photography, O'Sullivan was chosen to accompany King across the Great Basin for the following three years as official photographer.

Ferdinand V. Hayden was appointed geologist of the "United States Geographical and Geological Survey of the Territories" in 1871, having previously explored Kansas, Nebraska, and the Dakotas. Hayden had recognized the importance of documentation through photography to validate sketches, paintings, and written accounts. In 1870, he had invited William Henry Jackson to champion his values of conservation and preservation by photographing the land. In 1871, Hayden led the first scientific survey into the Yellowstone region. Again, Jackson was chosen as official photographer, and Thomas Moran joined the party as the official artist of the expedition. Coupled with the overwhelming success of the mission and the ensuing publicity, Jackson's photographs and Moran's paintings of the natural wonders of the area persuaded Congress in 1872, to pass the bill that established Yellowstone National Park.

In 1869, John Wesley Powell had led his crew of scientific explorers into the Grand Canyon through the Green and Colorado rivers without a photographer. However in 1871, when Lieutenant George Wheeler obtained government funds for exploration of the same area, he invited O'Sullivan to publicize and dramatize the expedition with photographs in order to demonstrate the military value of the expedition as well as the potential for economic exploitation of the region. The United States Geographical Surveys West of the 100th Meridian were Wheeler's response to the civilian surveys lead by Powell, King, and Hayden. After O'Sullivan accompanied the survey party up and down the Colorado River through the Grand Canyon, he was sent back to Washington with his photographs. Wheeler had hoped O'Sullivan's photographs might help persuade Congress to fund only military expeditions in the future. Although the photographer William Bell replaced O'Sullivan on Wheeler's second survey in 1872 through the Grand Canyon, O'Sullivan rejoined Wheeler's party in 1873 for the third survey. From this third survey, O'Sullivan's most noted photos documented Southwestern Indian and Spanish cultures.

In 1879, the United States Geological Survey was created in part to consolidate the former land surveys. Clarence King served as the bureau's first director for one year before Powell assumed leadership until 1894. Timothy O'Sullivan was the official photographer for the first year and a half. The purpose of the new organization, both then and now, was the geological exploration, mapping, and classification of public lands and the examination of geological structures and natural resources by a single government agency. Therefore, tension between military and civilian surveys as well as competition for financial backing ended, as all other surveys previously supported by the federal government were disbanded at the establishment of the United States Geological Survey.

Cory Pike

William Henry Jackson
Mountain of the Holy Cross. **1873**
Albumen print
7¼ x 9½ in
Colorado State Historical Society.

Mark Klett and Gordon Bushaw for the Rephotographic Survey Project
Mountain of the Holy Cross (after Jackson). **1978**
Silver print
7¼ x 9½ in
Courtesy of the Rephotographic Survey Project.

Andrew Russell
*Hanging Rock, Floor of Echo Cañon,
Utah.* c. 1867-68
Albumen print
6 x 7¾ in
R. Joseph and Elaine R. Monsen Collection.
Photo by Richard Nicol.

**Rick Dingus for the Rephotographic
Survey Project**
Hanging Rock (after Russell). 1978
Silver print
6 x 7¾ in
Courtesy of the Rephotographic Survey Project.

• William Henry Jackson
Whitehouse Mountain and Elk Lake.
1873
Albumen print
9 x 13 in
Collection of the U.S. Geological Survey.

• Mark Klett and JoAnn Verburg for the Rephotographic Survey Project
Snowmass Mountain and Geneva Lake.
1977
Silver print
9 x 13 in
Courtesy of the Rephotographic Survey Project.

Carleton Emmons Watkins
Malakoff Diggins, North Bloomfield,
Nevada County. c. 1871
Albumen print
16¾ x 21½ in
Collection of C. David Robinson. Photo courtesy
of Fraenkel Gallery.

94

William Henry Jackson
Cãnon of the Rio Las Animas. **c. 1882**
Albumen print
17$\frac{1}{16}$x20$\frac{7}{8}$ in
Colorado State Historical Society.

95

Laura Gilpin
Mesa. 1921
Platinum print
7 9/16 x 9 1/4 in

Collection, The Museum of Modern Art, New York,
Gift of Miss Mina Turner. Photograph copyright
1981 Laura Gilpin Collection, Amon Carter Museum,
Fort Worth, Texas.

John Vachon
Riding Out to Bring Back the Cattle,
First Stages of Snow Blizzard,
Lyman, South Dakota. 1940
Silver print
7 1/8 x 9 7/16 in

R. Joseph and Elaine R. Monsen Collection.
Photo by Richard Nicol.

97

Edward Weston
Sand Dunes, Oceano, California. **1936**
Gelatin silver print
7⅜ x 9¼ in
Center for Creative Photography, Tucson, Arizona.

100

Edward Weston
Quaker State Oil, Arizona. **1941**
Gelatin silver print
7⅝ x 9⅝ in
Collection, The Museum of Modern Art, New York.
Purchased as the gift of Mrs. Armand P. Bartos.
Photograph copyright Arizona Board of Regents,
Center for Creative Photography.

Robert Adams
Below Mt. Garfield, Mesa County,
Colorado (from the Missouri West
Portfolio). 1979
Silver print
13⁵⁄₁₆ x 8⅞ in
Seattle Art Museum, Gift of Byron Meyer.

Lewis Baltz
*Between West Sidewinder Drive and
State Highway 248, Looking North
(#13 from Park City Portfolio).* **1979**
Silver print
6$\frac{7}{16}$ x 9$\frac{1}{2}$ in
Henry Art Gallery, University of Washington, Seattle,
Monsen Study Collection of Photography, Gift of R.
Joseph and Elaine R. Monsen, 89.27.

Frank Gohlke
Mount St. Helens Shrouded In Its Own
Cloud—From Six Miles Northwest of
Mount St. Helens. 1983
Silver print
20 x 24 in
Courtesy of the artist.

Paul Caponigro
Monument Valley, Utah. **1970**
Silver print
10 x 13¾ in
Courtesy of the artist.

106

Len Jenshel
Goulding's Trading Post,
Monument Valley. **1987**
Ektacolor print
20 x 24 in
Courtesy, Laurence Miller Gallery, New York.

THE WESTERN HERO

Charles Russell. *Men of the Open Range*, c. 1922 (detail).
See page 124.

Frederic Remington
Fight for the Waterhole. 1901
Oil on canvas
27¼ x 40⅛ in
The Museum of Fine Arts, Houston,
The Hogg Brothers Collection,
Gift of Miss Ima Hogg.

Frederic Remington's West
Where History Meets Myth

Brian W. Dippie

"…Eastern people have formed their conceptions of what the Far-Western life is like, more from what they have seen in Mr. Remington's pictures than from any other source."[1]
William A. Coffin, 1892

Today we are conscious of the artfulness—and the artifice—in Frederic Remington's vision of the American West. It is a modern truism that Remington (1861-1909) invented the West of our imagination, the West of myth. It is worth remembering, however, that it was a truism in his day, and long after, that he was the Old West's most reliable reporter, "careful and trustworthy," an 1891 notice observed. "He draws only what he knows, and his knowledge can be relied on, even to small details."[2] His work might be faulted as art for its raw colors and unpoetic content. But it was almost always praised for its truthfulness. And thus the puzzle: How could Remington be both pictorial historian and supreme mythmaker? What was this West he had created where history met myth?

Remington had no trouble defining it. *His* West was "the West of picturesque and stirring events," of "romance and adventure." It was a fleeting moment that ended with the advent of civilization. "The typical figures of the plains," Remington told a reporter in 1907, were by then as extinct as the Paleozoic period. His West had passed "utterly out of existence so long ago as to make it merely a dream. It put on its hat, took up its blankets and marched off the board." Remington was not the only American around the turn of the century to use emotive language in discussing the frontier's demise. But even as a novice illustrator back in the 1880s he had seized on a theme with obsolescence built into it: the *winning* of the West, a process not a place. You could not visit Remington's West by boarding a train or retracing his steps. You could visit it only in works whose precise detail and unsparing realism offered assurance it had once actually existed. "He is the most conscientious of historians," the reporter who interviewed him in 1907 concluded. "He has never 'faked' an action, a costume or an episode."[3]

Yet much of Remington's work seems patently fabricated to modern eyes, and the artist himself was amused to remark the same year that people "take my pictures for veritable happenings and speculate on what will happen next" to the "puppets" he had placed in motion.[4] Was there some point in his career when he crossed a dividing line between history and myth? Was there a Remington, the documentary realist, who preceded Remington the imaginative artist? Was there a clear frontier between experience and make-believe that might account for his contrary reputations?

Remington's actual western experiences are not well documented. From a comfortable upstate New York family, he attended Yale's School of Fine Arts (1878-1879) before a small advance on his inheritance permitted a brief trip to Montana in 1881. Smitten, he returned West in 1883 after receiving the balance of his inheritance and bought a sheep ranch in Kansas, where he lived for about a year. Kansas City was next, 1884-1885—his longest stay in the West. Subsequently he contented himself with short visits on an almost annual basis while establishing his reputation as a western illustrator. He broke into print in 1882 with a depiction of Montana cowboys redrawn by an experienced illustrator and published in *Harper's Weekly* as *Cow-boys of Arizona: Roused by a Scout,* but did not appear on his own until the same periodical featured his *The Apache War: Indian Scouts on Geronimo's Trail* on January 9, 1886. Remington's direct, vigorous style captured eastern imaginations, and by decade's end he was already considered one of the West's foremost delineators. Assignments took him to Arizona to cover the Apache campaign, to Mexico and the Canadian plains, and to Dakota for the Ghost Dance outbreak that rang the curtain down on America's Indian wars.[5]

Even then, many of Remington's illustrations were based on hearsay, not firsthand experience. He patrolled with the cavalry indeed. But when he pictured combat with the Apaches or the fighting at Wounded Knee, he was relying on what he had heard, not seen. Early on he perfected the illustrator's knack of generalizing from personal knowledge, and had the power to create a fully realized world peopled by distinctive "types" engaged in characteristic activities. He had his self-reliant cowboys and wasp-waisted army officers down to an art. His Indians

111

The notes for the text begin on page 186.

were sullen, savage antidotes to romantic fantasies, and he added bullwhackers and prospectors and mountain men and a parade of others to his inventory of Westerners, "men with the bark on." Repetition, and his own earned credentials, validated what he showed even when he was depicting scenes from an era well before his time.

Indeed, the perimeters of his personal experience conveniently expanded with his reputation. Pressed by an interviewer in 1903 as to whether his work in fact all derived from firsthand observation, Remington replied cagily, "Not all," adding "I ranched… and got into Indian campaigns." This was true as far as it went. He had owned a sheep ranch, and had patrolled with the cavalry in Arizona and Dakota. But his interviewer understandably concluded more, writing that Remington once punched cows in Montana, "made money on a Kansas mule ranch, and was cowboy, guide, and scout in the Southwest."[6]

His 1907 interviewer just kept on embroidering: Remington "was once a ranger on the limitless prairies, a hard-riding, rough-living, free-fighting cowpuncher,—for do not lose sight of the fact that Frederic Remington has put himself and his own experiences in very nearly every picture he has drawn or painted. 'He rides like a Comanche,' said one of his friends…'He knows as much about horses and cattle as any man alive. And so he should, for he spent most of his youth in the saddle, rounding up mavericks, chasing and being chased by red men, and hobnobbing with scouts, pioneers, miners, and the picturesque freebooters of the plains."[7] Who would not surmise that the stage racing out of control with Indians in hot pursuit had Frederic Remington aboard? And who would not assume that he was squatted behind a rock in the foreground watching as a white officer helped rescue a fallen black soldier under galling fire from the ambuscaded enemy? Like the West he was portraying, Remington was his own invention. His experience corroborated the imaginary; the appearance of historical truth became truth itself. Remington seems to have made an effortless transition between history and myth, imbuing what was mostly mundane with a higher meaning. In his work, it was the meaning that mattered.

Remington's treatment of subject matter was uniformly realistic, and this consistency was key to the fusion between observation and invention. An illustration showing a cavalry patrol in the mountains looked the same as one showing the fight at Wounded Knee. A sketch of an Apache scout talking to a black trooper resembled one showing Apaches dragging a wounded trooper off for torture. Remington's rendering of cowboys saddling a skittish bronco was akin to one of a gunfight outside a saloon, his depiction of an Indian horse race to one of an encounter between soldiers and Indians. An illustration like *Steer-Hunting*, published in *Century Magazine*, August 1889, reads the same way as an oil like *The Fight for the Stolen Herd* (n.d.). Yet in each case the former was based on experience, the latter on imagination. What Remington saw and did validated what he did not see and did not do. But for his audience they were one and the same, and added up to Frederic Remington's distinctive vision of life in the West. "It is a fact that admits of no question that Eastern people have formed their conceptions of what the Far-Western life is like, more from what they have seen in Mr. Remington's pictures than from any other source," a critic observed as early as 1892.[8] The point was that Remington had been *"out there,"* Owen Wister, another mythmaker extraordinaire, explained, and had "made a page of American history his own."[9]

It was Wister also who commented on Remington's genius for creating the "typical": "Remington with his piercing and yet imaginative eye has taken the likeness of the modern American soldier and stamped it upon our minds with a blow as clean-cut as is the impression of the American Eagle upon our coins in the Mint."[10] He did more than soldiers. Remington sketches of western types published in *Century Magazine* over a four-year span—*A Montana Type*, the typical cowboy (March 1888), *The Sign Language*, the typical black soldier (April 1889), *Apache Soldier, or Scout* (July 1889), *"I Took Ye for an Injin,"* the typical mountain man (November 1890), and *A Typical Trooper*, the typical white soldier (July 1891)—offer generic figures in identical poses.

Frederic Remington
Fight for the Stolen Herd. **1908-09**
Oil on canvas
30 x 50 in
Museum of Western Art, Denver.

Frederic Remington
Steer Hunting.
Century Magazine, August, 1889
University of Washington Libraries.

• Frederic Remington
The Last Stand.
Harper's Weekly, January 10, 1891

• A. R. Waud
Custer's Last Fight.
From Frederick Whittaker's *A Popular Life of General George A. Custer,* 1876.

114

An 1890 painting of troopers at bay desperately fight-ing an unseen enemy was published as *The Last Stand* in *Harper's Weekly,* January 10, 1891, along with an editorial note that asked: "How many scenes of which this is typical have been enacted on this continent, who can say?"[11] The correct answer, in truth, was not many, despite the fame of Custer's Last Stand. But the implication was that Remington had merely recorded a commonplace of the Indian wars, a bit of misleading propaganda made doubly ironic by the picture's appearance as a two-page spread twelve days after the tragedy at Wounded Knee. An Indian last stand would have been more "typical" of western history, but Remington was merely making a contribution toward his over-riding theme, the winning of the West.

Myth, then, and not history was the essence of a scene whose unblinking realism argued otherwise. Indeed, *The Last Stand* had an interesting pedigree. As a teenager, Remington made a colored sketch of *Custer's Last Fight,* ca. 1877, based on one of the ear-liest published versions by A. R. Waud. The image stuck in his head, and Waud's distinctive grouping —purely imaginary—is still evident in *The Last Stand* and in a Remington black and white oil published in 1903 as *Custer's Last Fight* in which the typical reverts to the specific. "One by one the soldiers fell," the accompanying editorial note this time explained, until Custer, "saber in hand, after killing three Indians, was shot dead."[12] And so the typical, rooted in myth not history, became part of Remington's mythical "historical" West.

• Frederic Remington
Return of the Blackfoot War Party.
1887
Oil on canvas
28 x 50 in
The Anschutz Collection, Denver.

• Frederic Remington
Thanksgiving Dinner for the Ranch.
Harper's Weekly, **November 24, 1888**

What is evident is that Remington's earliest published illustrations do not differentiate between the documentary and the imaginary. Moreover, even as Remington worked in black and white for the magazines, he was out to make his mark as an easel painter. He exhibited as early as 1888, held his first one-man show in 1890, and throughout his career would strive for acceptance as an artist as opposed to an illustrator. His first major bid for recognition, *Return of the Blackfoot War Party,* 1887, was entered in the National Academy of Design exhibition for 1888. It shows a young Remington at his most self-conscious as he tried to make art out of his western experiences. The composition, and atmosphere, can be linked to an illustration published later that year on November 24, 1888, in *Harper's Weekly, Thanksgiving Dinner for the Ranch.* By substituting Indians for cowboys, Remington gained an exoticism acceptable to a generation that had made Orientalism a staple of the academies, while adding a poignant story element—miserable prisoners being herded through the snow—quite in line with the conventions of history painting. Obviously he had witnessed no such scene out West. The painting worked in costume bits that he had admired—and acquired—on a trip to Canada, but the subject resided purely in Remington's imagination where art—as distinct from illustration—was supposed to dwell. The cowboys could be accepted as history, the Blackfoot as myth.

Remington also used his factual knowledge to nonfactual ends in other major early paintings. The oil *A Cavalryman's Breakfast on the Plains,* ca. 1892 looks like a straightforward document. In fact, it too is cobbled together from various documentary bits. One figure in that group of troopers on the left grooming themselves or bent over the cookfire appeared twice in illustrations published in *Harper's Weekly* in 1892: *Cooking in Camp—The Galloping Sixth* (January 16) and *Roasting the Christmas Beef in a Cavalry Camp* (December 24). The soldier with the towel over his shoulder served Remington as an interchangeable part. So did the figure of the scout reporting to the officers on the right, derived from *Ben. Clark, Interpreter* which appeared in *Century Magazine,* August 1889. To this point Remington would seem to have done no great violence to his sources. But that central cluster of officers is another matter. It is based on a sketch of black troopers that

Remington published in *Century Magazine,* April 1889, as *A Campfire Sketch.* He might ride with the black Tenth Cavalry ("the 10th Nubian Horse," as he characteristically put it), and he might admire their stamina, fighting spirit, and dedication to duty.[13] But Remington's West was a white man's country, and black soldiers would play almost no part in his major oils. So history whitened into myth.

If some of Remington's earlier oils reveal a conscious progression from history to myth, his 20th-century oils would seem entirely mythological. Frustrated by the denial of critical recognition, he sought to reorient his work. He had always responded to the West in terms of the colorful first, and its actual colors only secondarily. That is, he had placed the actors—his men with the bark on, his western types—front and center, making the setting a minimalist backdrop to the human drama. Now he responded to the land itself, light, color, atmosphere, integrating his figures into the setting. "I have studied form so much that I never had a chance to 'let go' and find if I can see with *the wide open eyes of a child,*" he wrote late in 1900 on the eve of his departure for a West he now found devoid of pictorial interest. "What I know has been pounded into me—I had to know it—now I am going to see…."[14] To some this has seemed to demarcate the borderline in Remington's work when he moved away from story to a concern with pure painting. But had he, in repudiating the role of illustrator, also repudiated his obsession with factual accuracy? Had he knowingly crossed from history into myth?

There is much to corroborate a psychological transformation in Remington corresponding to the transition between centuries. Remington turned forty in 1901. His youth, like the Wild West that had symbolized the nation's youth, was finished, and he was too old to go on playing cowboy, or cowboy illustrator. "Shall never come west again," he wrote his wife late in 1900 from Santa Fe. "It is all brick buildings—derby hats and blue overhauls—it spoils my early illusions—and they are *my* capital."[15] Remington craved critical recognition that he had matured as an artist; by and large, before his death in December 1909, he had got it. His last exhibition, which closed at M. Knoedler's in New York on December 11, 1909, was a triumph. The reviewers had all come down to praise him as a "mere painter," he wrote in his diary

shortly before he died. "I have been on their trail a long while and they never surrendered while they had a leg to stand on. The 'Illustrator' phase has become a background."[16] Remington's judgment has entrenched itself in recent scholarship. He is assessed in light of his artistic contemporaries and by his skills as painter and (after 1895) sculptor. Critics downplay content, emphasize stylistic progression, and confirm the impression that after 1900 the erstwhile pictorial historian of the West was just another, albeit highly talented, American artist.

In our desire to give Remington his artistic due we risk substituting one set of limitations for another. Simply, we cannot ignore the continuing importance of subject matter in his art. He himself served notice in his last year: "I stand for the proposition of 'subjects'—painting something worth while as against painting *nothing* well—merely *paint.*"[17] His affinities with nonwestern artists are essential to any understanding of his achievement. But no influence on Remington the artist was greater than Remington the illustrator. That is why contemporary critics continued to see him as different. Attuned as they were to trends and nuances, and able to read altered agendas, they persisted in viewing Remington as distinctive because of his subjects irrespective of his treatment of them. He remained to them a western artist, and while such labeling would seem anathema to the "new" Remington, he willingly accepted it. "I am," he said in 1907, "now painting the things which I saw as a boy or things which I heard about from men who took active part in the stir of the early West."[18]

Many of Remington's 20th-century oils have roots in earlier illustrations. Some were direct adaptations. His sketch *Bronco Busters Saddling (Century Magazine,* February 1888) reappeared as *His First Lesson,* 1903, with the subtle changes common to Remington's later work as he implied limits on the once limitless West in the adobe buildings behind and the shadow cast across the foreground by the corral gate. An oil sketch like *Ghost Riders,* ca. 1909 is proof positive that lurking within Remington's mature paintings are often the ghostly forms of illustrations past. Impressionistic and allegorical, it nevertheless draws on his very literal rendition of a pair of Indian riders, *Two Fleeting Ghosts I Saw,* published in *Harper's Weekly* for January 31, 1891.[19]

• **Frederic Remington**
Ghost Riders. c. 1909
Oil on board
12 x 18 in
Courtesy of the Buffalo Bill Historical Center,
Cody, Wyoming.

• **Frederic Remington**
Two Fleeting Ghosts I Saw.
Harper's Weekly, January 31, 1891

• **Frederic Remington**
A Campfire Sketch.
Century Magazine, April, 1889

• **Frederic Remington**
A Cavalryman's Breakfast on the
Plains. 1892
Oil on canvas
22 x 32⅛ in
Amon Carter Museum, Fort Worth.

• **Frederic Remington**
Moonlight Scouting Party. **c. 1907**
The Thomas Gilcrease Institute of American History and Art, Tulsa, Oklahoma.

• **Frederic Remington**
The Sign Language.
Century Magazine, **August, 1889**

• **Frederic Remington**
A Taint in the Wind. **1906**
Oil on canvas
28⅛ x 40 in
Sid W. Richardson Collection, Fort Worth.

• **Frederic Remington**
The Right of the Road. **1900**
Oil on canvas
27¼ x 40¼ in
Amon Carter Museum, Fort Worth.

In particular, Remington turned day into night to create heightened tension and a sense of pathos and foreboding in his later work. *Waiting for the Beef Issue (Century Magazine,* August 1889) assumes a very different meaning when the same figures are shown as a *Moonlight Scouting Party,* ca. 1907. "Big art," Remington remarked in 1903, "is a process of elimination. Cut down and out—…let your audience take away something to think about—to imagine."[20] Hold back some of the story, in short, as one did not do in illustration. Nocturnes lent themselves to such minimalism. They were evocative mood pieces, startling figures into tense poses, cloaking a West become mundane in the mysteries of moonlight and shadow, and in them Remington perfected the art of cutting down. The horses in *The Right of the Road,* 1900 are recoiling from nothing more exciting than a bicycler in the foreground; the identical team in the nocturne *A Taint in the Wind,* 1906 are responding to an unseen *something,* harmless or threatening Remington does not say, leaving the source of their alarm to the viewer's imagination. Again, progression in Remington's artistry is a developmental sequence involving external influences, certainly, but also internal ones, evident in the self-referential nature of many of his major works. The persistence of the illustrator in the mature artist is one reason why the borderline between history and myth in Remington's work is so elusive.

To establish the ongoing importance of illustration to Remington's most imaginative pieces, one need only consider two of his overt experiments in pure color. *Indian, Horse, and Village,* 1907, with its plain-spoken title and mystical aura, derives its basic composition from a seemingly unrelated illustration of a cowboy, *The Herd at Night (Century Magazine,* April 1888). In both, a horseback figure, seen from the rear, is placed against wedges of darkness and light. The one is descriptive, the other ethereal, a point more evident in comparing *The Sign Language (Century Magazine,* August 1889) and *The Gossips,* 1909. The two Indians engaged in conversation in the black-and-white illustration reappeared in a flood of oranges and browns to continue their discussion twenty years later. Much in the way of artistic growth separated the two gossiping pairs, but the original inspiration was essentially unaltered. In tonalist works like *Indian, Horse, and Village* and *The Gossips,*

myth would appear to have completely displaced history, yet the documentary remains embedded in the purely artistic, supporting Royal Cortissoz's judgment after viewing the last Remington exhibition: "He is, then, both historian and artist."[21]

It is indisputable that Remington's artistic goals changed in the 20th century. But even as he explored new directions in his work, he was reluctant to relinquish old standards of factual accuracy and his title as the West's foremost painter. His attack on Charles Schreyvogel in 1903 is a case in point. Schreyvogel, a German-trained Hoboken, New Jersey, artist had been getting under Remington's skin for some time. He was not just painting the West too; he was stealing Remington's ideas—and thunder. In 1900 he committed the unpardonable sin of winning the coveted Thomas B. Clarke Prize of the National Academy of Design for *My Bunkie,* an oil clearly derived from Remington's 1896 bronze *The Wounded Bunkie.* Denied such academic recognition himself, Remington was irate. Others, he darkly hinted to Owen Wister, were trying to cut in, pretending that "they too understand."[22]

His opportunity to strike back came in 1903 with the well-publicized unveiling of Schreyvogel's latest historical oil, *Custer's Demand,* depicting an 1869 parley between soldiers and Indians. More poaching: Remington had done some Custer subjects in the past, and had been cranking up for a major work on the theme "for years." He might have attacked *Custer's Demand* on artistic grounds. The composition was static, the background figures stuck on. Instead he denounced it for its historical inaccuracy as "half-baked stuff" and proceeded to list Schreyvogel's factual errors. Nothing escaped his notice. Pistol holders, ammunition belts, warbonnets, hats, boots, stirrup covers, saddlebags, saddle cloths, uniform colors, even the height of Custer's horse—all wrong, all unauthentic, and thus all bad. The denouement: an army officer present at the parley, General Custer's widow, even President Theodore Roosevelt, rushed to Schreyvogel's defense, and Remington was left to limp away, looking foolish.[23]

The Schreyvogel affair is usually cited to show a petty streak in Remington, but of more significance is that he still *cared.* At a time when he was noisily proclaiming a sea change in his artistic priorities, Remington was busy drawing lines around his turf,

his West, and fending off interlopers. This was a Remington who had not rejected his illustrator's past to embrace the artist's higher calling. This was a Remington still jealous of his original fame. It "wasn't because I knew how to draw that I met with my first success," he explained, "for I didn't, but because I knew the West better than any other man."[24] As late as 1903 he was still prepared to make that boast, though after his clash with Schreyvogel, he never again placed so much emphasis on factual accuracy as a criterion for artistic merit. The mood, the impression, light, color, and the larger meanings of the West became his obsessions, and he experimented with nonwestern subjects as well. But in the 20th century he was prisoner to the public perception he had once labored to foster: for most Americans, he remained the ultimate western realist. The tributes following his death in 1909 sounded a familiar refrain. "His young manhood was spent in the far West, at work with the cow-boys and near the soldiers and Indians whose picture historian he was destined to become," Augustus Thomas wrote.[25] His work, Leonard Wood added, is "technically and historically accurate, and as such forms, and will ever form, a true picture of the West, of the cowboy, the Indian, and the plainsman as they were."[26]

As for the distinction between history and myth, there had never been a firm borderline for Remington. From the beginning he was creating an alternate reality, his West. Perhaps he succeeded too well. People everywhere mistook it for the actual thing, praising Remington not for the imaginative power, the vision, the artistry required to create it, but for literally, faithfully, unimaginatively recording simply what was. Frederic Remington's greatest creation, his West, had become a commonplace, and his myth, an accepted part of American history.

Brian W. Dippie, professor of history at the University of Victoria, British Columbia, is a specialist in 19th-century American history and Western American literature and art. He is the author of *Remington and Russell: The Sid Richardson Collection, Looking at Russell,* and the forthcoming *Catlin and His Contemporaries: The Politics of Patronage.*

120

Frederic Remington
Ghosts of the Past. c. 1908
Oil on canvas
12 x 16 in
Courtesy of the Buffalo Bill Historical Center,
Cody, Wyoming.

Frederic Remington
The Cowboy. **1902**
Oil on canvas
40¼ x 27⅛ in
Amon Carter Museum, Fort Worth.
Photo by Linda Lorenz.

123

Charles Russell
Men of the Open Range. c. 1923
Oil on canvas
24 x 36 in
Montana State Historical Society,
MacKay Collection, Helena, Montana.

Charles Russell's Home Turf

It is difficult to imagine how raw and unsettled Montana Territory was when Russell arrived there. There were no transcontinental railroads in Montana in 1880. The one narrow-gauge line over which Charlie had made part of his trip had barely crossed the southern boundary of the Territory the preceding September. Most of the travel from "the States" then, and for another ten years, was by steamboat up the Missouri to the head of navigation at Fort Benton. From there the wayfarers waited for an uncertain stage to the mining camps, or traveled by horseback to other destinations.

Indian wars were still a vivid memory to many Montanans in 1880. Custer and most of his Seventh Cavalry had been wiped out only four years earlier and Chief Joseph and his tribe of fighting Nez Percé had been beaten and captured only three years before. The vast area north of the Marias and Missouri rivers and from the Continental Divide east to the Dakota line was "Indian country," set aside as a reservation for the Blackfoot Indians and their allies. Another large area south of the Yellowstone River was the home of the Crow.

Aside from the military forts, settlements of other kinds were few and far between. Most of the more important of these were mining camps. Helena, the largest, had become the territorial capital, boasting of a population of seven thousand persons in 1880. The roistering camp of Butte had less than half the number and most of the others a few hundred or less. "Great Falls" was only a waterfall on the Missouri River, the town of that name not yet existent.

In the great interior east of the Rockies were the beginnings of a few scattered ranches although the hills were still "black with buffalo" in some areas. It was to be another two years before the last great Indian buffalo hunt of 1882. Game was abundant everywhere and buffalo tongue, roast venison, and saddle of antelope were standard items on the menus of the stage stations and the few other public eating places. This was the country Charlie Russell saw, fell in love with, and made his home in for the next forty-six years.

Charlie had his first job herding sheep in the Judith Basin. In describing his early days in Montana some years later, Charlie wrote:

I did not stay as long as the sheep and I did not get along well, but I do not think my employer missed me much, as I was considered pretty ornery. I soon took up with a hunter and trapper named Jake Hoover. This life suited me. We had six horses, a saddle apiece, and pack animals. I stayed about two years with Hoover, when I had to go back to St. Louis. I brought back a cousin of mine who died of mountain fever two weeks after we arrived. When I pulled out of Billings I had four bits in my pockets and 200 miles between me and Hoover. There was much snow, as it was April, but after riding about fifteen miles I struck a cow outfit coming in to receive 1,000 dougies for the 12 Z and V outfit up the basin. The boss, John Cabler, hired me to night-wrangle horses. We were about a month on the trail and turned loose on Ross Fork, where we met the Judith roundup. They had just fired their night herder and Cabler gave me a good word, so I took the herd. It was a lucky thing no one knew me or I never would have had the job.

I was considered pretty worthless, but in spite of that fact I held their bunch, which consisted of 200 saddle horses. That same fall old True hired me to night herd his beef, and for 11 years I sung to the horses and cattle.

During these eleven years Charlie was painting and sketching at every possible moment. At the first light of day a man was sent out to relieve the night herder, and after getting back to camp Charlie had his daytime hours pretty much to himself. After getting a few hours of sleep, Charlie had the rest of the day to watch as the crew worked and branded the herd, while he made quick sketches.

In the first part of this period it is doubtful that Charlie had any notion of eventually earning his living as an artist. He was painting and sketching for his own amusement, giving away the results of his efforts to anyone, friend or stranger, who admired them. Most of these went to his cowboy friends and were tacked up on bunkhouse walls.

His first formal commission was from James Shelton, a saloon man of Utica, Montana. Shelton wanted a decoration to hang behind his bar and approached Charlie with a request that he paint something that would interest his patrons. Charlie had neither canvas nor other materials and there was no place in the Judith Basin where he could buy them. A smooth pine slab nearly seven feet long and a foot and a half wide served for a canvas and his oils were presumably house paints.

In the winter of 1885 Charlie completed what was at that time his largest oil painting on canvas. This was a lively scene, eighteen by thirty-six inches in size, of the Utica roundup crew. Charlie called the painting *Breaking Camp*. Without mentioning it to anyone, he sent the painting off to be shown at the St. Louis Art Exposition of 1886. This was Russell's first painting to be exhibited outside the state of Montana.

Charlie continued his life as a cowboy until 1893. As he put it, "That fall, after work was over I left [the range] and I never sang to the horses and cattle again."

With the end of the roundup that year, Charlie was one of the cowboys selected to accompany the beef train to Chicago. After spending a few days taking in the sights of the World's Fair, he continued on to St. Louis to visit his parents. While there, Charlie called on William Niedringhaus, a prominent St. Louis hardware merchant, who also had ranching interests in Montana. The outcome of the visit to the Niedringhaus home in St. Louis was a commission for several paintings, the price unspecified and the choice of subject entirely Charlie's.

It was undoubtedly this commission that led Charlie to give up his life as a cowboy. Although he had previously sold a number of his paintings, the income from such sales had been both small and irregular. Charlie probably decided that here was the opportunity to find out whether he could earn his living as an artist.

Reprinted by permission of the publisher Harry N. Abrams, Inc., New York, from the book *Charles M. Russell* by Frederic G. Renner (New York: Abradale Press and Harry N. Abrams in association with the Amon Carter Museum of Western Art, Fort Worth, Texas, 1966, rev. ed., 1984).

Charles Russell
Friend Bill. 1924
Pen and ink, watercolor, opaque white and
graphite on paper
10⅛ x 8 in
Amon Carter Museum, Fort Worth.

Charles Russell
Waiting for a Chinook. 1886
Watercolor on paper
3 x 4 in
Montana Stockgrowers Association,
Helena, Montana.

Charles Russell
Making a Cigarette (former title:
The Virginian). c. 1911
Pen and ink on paper
12⅝ x 9⅝ in
Amon Carter Museum, Fort Worth.

In 1886, severe, unrelenting winter storms held Montana in
an icy grip that would ruin the cattle industry for years to
come, and serve as one of the junctures that heralded the
end of the old Wild West. Charles Russell painted the simple watercolor, *Waiting for a Chinook,* 1886 on a scrap of
cardboard torn from a collar box. It was sent as a reply to an
owner's request for a report on the condition of his herd of
five thousand cattle.

Charles Russell
Breaking Camp. c. 1885
Oil on canvas
18½ x 36⅛ in
Amon Carter Museum, Fort Worth.

Charles Russell
Wildman's Truce. **1914**
Oil on canvas
24 x 36 in
Courtesy of the National Cowboy Hall of Fame,
Oklahoma City, Oklahoma.

128

Charles Russell
Carson's Men. **1913**
Oil on canvas
24 x 35½ in
The Thomas Gilcrease Institute of American History
and Art, Tulsa, Oklahoma.

129

Charles Russell
The Hold Up. **1899**
Oil on canvas
30⅛ x 48⅛ in
Amon Carter Museum, Fort Worth.
Photo by Linda Lorenz.

130

This painting depicts the holdup of the Miles City, Montana, to Bismarck, South Dakota, stage by Big Nose George, an outlaw who operated in the Black Hills country in the early 1880s. The passengers are a cross section of frontier characters—a clergyman, a prospector, a schoolmarm, a gambler, a Chinese, the widow Flannagan, who ran the Miles City boardinghouse, and Mr. Isaac Katz, who had come west from New York City to open a clothing store. Just prior to this event, Mr. Katz had several thousand dollars sewn in his clothes, an unsuccessful strategy as we see here.

Charles Russell
La Vérendryes Discover the Rocky Mountains. c. 1911
Pen and ink, and graphite on paper
14 x 22¼ in
Amon Carter Museum, Fort Worth.

Charles Russell
Killing of Jules Remi by Slade. c. 1922
Pen and ink, and graphite on paper
14 x 22 in
Amon Carter Museum, Fort Worth.

Sieur de La Vérendrye was one of France's bold voyagers in search of the Northwest Passage. In 1743, during his search for the mythical waterway, the explorer and his two sons came upon a shimmering range at a point in present-day Wyoming. They called the range the "Shining Mountains," and became the first Europeans to look at the Northern Rockies.

Frank Tenney Johnson
Thornburgh's Battlefield. **1934**
Oil on canvas
40½ x 50½ in
Archer M. Huntington Gallery, the University of
Texas at Austin, Gift of C. R. Smith, 1976.
Photo by George Holmes.

Frank Tenney Johnson
A Fresh Mount. **1932**
Oil on canvas
36¼ x 46 in
Amon Carter Museum, Fort Worth.

In 1879 near the Milk River in Colorado, two hundred soldiers commanded by Major Thomas T. Thornburgh fought more than three hundred Ute Indians in a week-long struggle. The skirmish began accidentally with an ill-conceived attempt by the United States government to bring agrarian practices to the Utes on the White River Reservation. This battle, along with the murder of a U.S. Indian agent on the reservation, became the U.S. government's final justification for banishing almost all of the Utes to a reservation in Utah.

133

The Pony Express was founded April 3, 1860, and provided mail service from Missouri to California until October 1861, when the telegraph took over as the primary means of communication. The Pony Express fee was one dollar per letter. Service to Salt Lake City was guaranteed in 124 hours, to Carson City in 188 hours, and to San Francisco in 240 hours.

Olaf Seltzer
A Dude's Welcome. 1909
Oil on canvas
18 x 24⅛ in
Amon Carter Museum, Fort Worth.

Between 1933 and 1935 Olaf Seltzer painted over one
hundred oils, not exceeding six inches in height or width,
depicting some of the most dramatic events in the history
of Montana. Seltzer's patron, the voracious art collector Phillip
Cole, requested that the works be so small because he had
already covered most of his mansion's interior walls with
paintings. Seltzer's eyesight was extremely impaired from
painting the miniatures.

Olaf Seltzer
Robber's Rock—Near Bannock,
Montana. Rendezvous for the
Plummer Gang of Road Agents.
c. 1933-35
Oil on board
3⅞ x 5¼ in
The Thomas Gilcrease Institute of American History
and Art, Tulsa, Oklahoma.

Olaf Seltzer
Execution of George Ives, Dec. 21,
1863—Nevada City, Madison County,
Montana. **1934**
Oil on board
5 x 6¼ in
The Thomas Gilcrease Institute of American History
and Art, Tulsa, Oklahoma.

Olaf Seltzer
The Vigilantes' Oath Organization
Meeting in Virginia City, Montana,
December 23, 1863. **1934**
Oil on board
6⅛ x 4⅛ in
The Thomas Gilcrease Institute of American History
and Art, Tulsa, Oklahoma.

135

Olaf Seltzer
Battle of Bear Paw—September 30 to October 4, 1877. c. 1933-35
Oil on board
4¼ x 6⅜ in
The Thomas Gilcrease Institute of American History and Art, Tulsa, Oklahoma.

Olaf Seltzer
The Pow Wow. 1935
Oil on board
4¼ x 6⅜ in
The Thomas Gilcrease Institute of American History and Art, Tulsa, Oklahoma.

Olaf Seltzer
The Hayfield Fight—August 1, 1867.
2,500 Sioux Defeated by 19 White
Men. **c. 1933-35**
Oil on board
4 x 6 in
The Thomas Gilcrease Institute of American History
and Art, Tulsa, Oklahoma.

137

On June 25, 1876, General George Armstrong Custer disregarded a Cheyenne warning and led his five companies of the Seventh Cavalry into battle with the Sioux on the hills overlooking the Little Bighorn River, in south-central Montana. Not one of the 210 members of Custer's command survived. This devastating defeat must have come as an incredible shock to a nation about to celebrate its centennial, but it has stayed in the public memory at least in part due to dramatic works of art such as Edgar S. Paxson's *Custer's Last Stand,* completed in December 1899, after almost two decades of research. Paxson took great care in attempting an accurate portrayal of the scene, and positioned his subjects in the painting according to where they fell. He referred to the markers on the battlefield and to his correspondence with General Edward S. Godfrey, who was among Captain Benteen's "K" Troop who would first discover the bodies.

Among the figures, Custer stands prominently in the upper center of the painting. He wears the buckskin suit and pearl-handled revolver described in detail in General Godfrey's letter of January 16, 1896, to the artist. His hair, which he commonly wore long, is shown cropped short, a precaution he took shortly before the battle, presumably to make his scalp less attractive to the enemy. Adjutant W. W. Cooke kneels on one knee immediately behind General Custer.

To the left and a little farther up Custer Hill is the general's brother, Captain Tom Custer, in a buckskin shirt open in the front. He fires one Colt revolver while cocking the other over his shoulder. Paxson also portrayed the unreliability of the Seventh Cavalry's rifles, and in the lower center of the painting a soldier can be seen anxiously trying to eject a jammed cartridge from his rifle with a knife.

Near Tom Custer, the mounted likeness of the young Sioux Rain-in-the-Face is about to strike the captain down from behind, avenging a long-time grudge. He would later boast that he cut out and ate the soldier's heart.

To the right of Rain-in-the-Face is General Custer's personal battle flag of intricately embroidered yellow silk: the flag he had gained at Lee's surrender at Appomattox. Paxson did not paint this flag into the picture until 1908, after General Godfrey remarked on its absence from the painting during a visit to the artist's studio to see the completed work. Farther right is the Seventh Cavalry's purple satin banner.

In the distant right is a cavalryman mounted on a light gray horse and receiving a bullet. This is Lieutenant James Calhoun, Custer's brother-in-law, who had apparently been riding toward Custer Hill from his initial position when shot. None of the other soldiers is shown mounted because it was the opinion of General Godfrey that Custer had ordered a dismount and removal to the rear of the horses at the outset of the battle.

Custer's half-breed scout Mitch Boyer is at right-center, clad in a buckskin suit with a feather in his hat. He fires his rifle at the oncoming figure of Crazy Horse, who, bearing the well-known scar on his cheek, raises a three-pronged war club. Below Crazy Horse, crouched low on a captured mount bearing the brand of the U.S. Cavalry, is the Uncapapa Sioux chief, Crow King.

Two Moon, a Cheyenne who later befriended Paxson and described the battle in detail to him on the battlefield while they camped there together, is at the far left. Only his warbonneted head and right hand holding a lance can be seen as he forces his pony into the fray.

In the left background, mounted on a white horse and directing the battle with an upraised right hand holding a rifle, is the Sioux war chief, Gall. He, too, in later years discussed the battle with the artist at the scene of the event.

This material is adapted from William Edgar Paxson, *E. S. Paxson, Frontier Artist* (Boulder, Colorado: Pruett Publishing Company, 1984), 43-48, 52-53. Reprinted with permission from William Edgar Paxson.

Edgar S. Paxson
Custer's Last Stand. **1899**
Oil on canvas
70½ x 106 in
Courtesy of the Buffalo Bill Historical Center,
Cody, Wyoming.
Photo by Douglas M. Parker.

Unknown
World's Wondrous Voyages. c. 1892
Color lithograph poster
27⅞ x 38½ in
Courtesy of the Buffalo Bill Historical Center,
Cody, Wyoming.

140

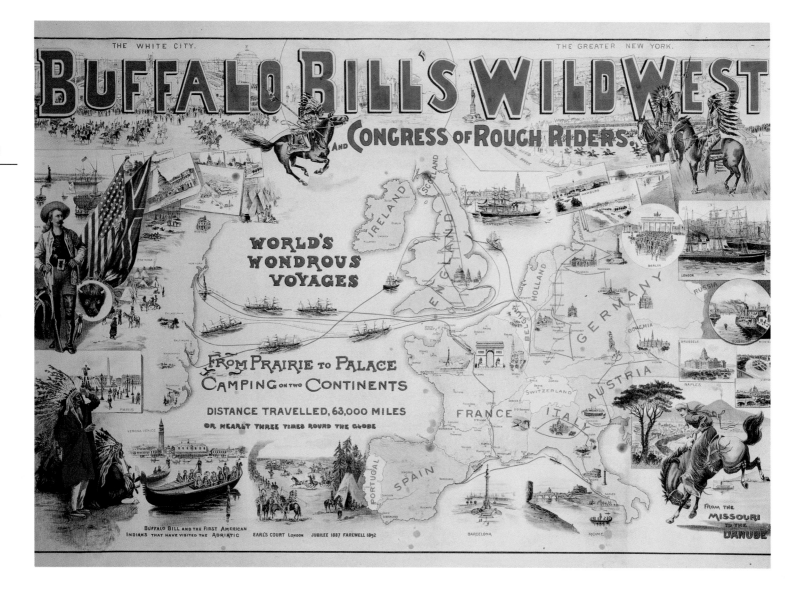

In Defense of Buffalo Bill
A Look at Cody in and of His Time

Paul Fees

"Buffalo Bill, Ned Buntline and Frederic Reming-ton… It is something to have created a region as large as the American West, and lo! have not these three done that thing?"[1]

Emerson Hough, 1909

Since William F. Cody's death in 1917, on the eve of American entry into World War I, scholars and critics have been trying to sort out the meanings of Buffalo Bill. Many of our cinematic stereotypes of the heroic West—the cowboy, the stagecoach, the warbonneted warrior, the blue-coated cavalry—had their begin-nings in Buffalo Bill's Wild West show. As boy on the plains, hunter, army scout, Indian fighter, showman, and entrepreneur, Buffalo Bill better than anybody symbolized the winning of the West. That is, he embodied and in his Wild West show simplified the narrative myth of the winning of the West.

It was a myth that in Cody's day helped unify a divided America with its celebration of individual heroic values and collective national accomplish-ment. It was expansive, forward-looking, and progres-sive, and Cody was its perfect exponent. He was flamboyant, successful, and had been a genuine frontier hero made larger-than-life by events. His audiences did not need to be reminded of who he was or the value of what he stood for. And it is in part because he was universally acknowledged to be the exemplary frontiersman that the myth itself was so uncritically embraced.

Nowadays, the array of images associated with the name makes his symbolism as ambivalent as the issues we try to explain through the myth he repre-sents. Increasingly, he and his West have come to stand for certain failures in American life, and Buffalo Bill has been made to fit into differing, even competing, myths of exploitation or social conflict.

The excesses of racism, for example, in America are easily and often interpreted in light of the treatment of Indians. Ecological blunders are best symbolized for many by the demise of the great buffalo herds. That Americans are fascinated with violence—a notion abetted by a highly visible gun culture fringe—is reinforced by popular conceptions of America's western past. Perhaps most damning in a dangerous world, the United States seems still to practice a frontier diplomacy—providing rations to the tribes on the reservation, punishing the ones that stray, using the "friendlies" against the "hostiles."

The myth of the West, in this view, has trapped America in a past that it must disavow. Its visible reminders—the western paintings of Frederic Remington, for example—must be considered for their mythic content rather than appreciated for their merits. Its symbols must be redefined in terms of current malaises.

The debunking of Buffalo Bill is linked to the reevaluation of our western myth. "He has made the American name respected throughout the world; the world is better for his living in this age," wrote a news-paper editor in 1896.[2] Yet recently a writer in the *New Haven Register* commented that Cody represented a "fraudulent mythologizing of greed and corruption."[3] Less than a century separates those comments and their world views. More often than not, as symbol, Cody is defined as a master of "the sleight-of-hand blurring of life and theater," a shaman and showman "whose lasting invention was his own part real, part fictitious identity."[4] So Buffalo Bill must be both a slaughterer of Indians and buffalo and at the same time an invention of press and public relations.

Purporting to speak with authority, an Iowa histo-rian recently claimed, "We're learning that Buffalo Bill was a very average person who, by his own promotion, transformed himself into an international figure of mythic proportions."[5]

But to assume that sheer press agentry could create and sustain Buffalo Bill trivializes both myth in general and the myth of the West in particular. Myth is a narrative, factual or fictional, that is power-ful enough to help us define what kind of people we are and subtle enough to be internalized. We don't have to think about it; we just know it.

The "winning of the West" is made up of many narrative symbols. Americans may not be proud of some—those that are interpreted as racist or imperialistic, for example. But those are only single elements in a much larger and more complex myth, a myth of accomplishment, of nation building, and in fact of unity.

And W. F. Cody was not by any measure an average person with ordinary experiences. It is precisely because he was genuine that his star outshone so many other self-proclaimed witnesses to the passing of the frontier. The role he occupied as symbol and principal narrator of the myth for more than forty years made him one of the best known men of his

The notes for the text begin on page 187.

age, on two continents. His contemporaries knew the events of Cody's life intuitively, but it becomes necessary for us to recite them, without skepticism.

He was born in 1846 in a log cabin a few miles west of the Mississippi in Iowa. It was the "Year of Decision," as Bernard DeVoto called it, when the United States fought Mexico in the Southwest and pushed England out of Oregon and decided to be a continental nation. Cody died seventy-one years later as the nation was making its decision to become a global power.[6]

In between, Cody was on hand for most of the iconic western events—gold rushes and wagon trains, Pony Express, trapping, railroad building, "cowboying" on the open range, the plains Indian wars. He was an active participant in most of them. His father was a restless westering man, and young Cody grew up among the Indians, the emigrants, and the frontiersmen near Fort Leavenworth, Kansas. As a member of the Seventh Kansas Volunteer Cavalry, he saw action as a Union soldier in America's greatest event, the Civil War. In 1866 he married a St. Louis girl, Louisa Frederici, and moved her west.

At twenty-one he earned his nickname, Buffalo Bill, because of his success providing fresh meat for railway crews building the Union Pacific across the plains of Kansas. Winning a nickname was no insignificant matter, and frontiersmen wore theirs like titles of nobility.[7] Only one of several Buffalo Bills in 1868 (one of them would be hanged as a horse thief), Cody soon became the only Buffalo Bill who mattered.[8]

The Indian wars provided the arena where Cody won his greatest acclaim. Warfare had been virtually continuous since the Appalachian frontier was breached a hundred years earlier. Pushed by an almost messianic zeal to make the wilderness economically productive, Americans continued to provoke confrontations over land ownership. The completion of the transcontinental railroad in the late 1860s exacerbated hostilities. With only twenty-six hundred regular soldiers to keep peace on the prairies, the army relied to a great extent on the plainscraft of civilians like Buffalo Bill.

His career as a scout in the decade after the Civil War would be unsurpassed, even by such legendary frontiersmen as Yellowstone Kelly, Halfbreed Frank Grouard, Big Bat Pourier, Little Bat Garnier, Texas Jack Omohundro, California Joe Milner, Medicine Bill Comstock, Lonesome Charley Reynolds, Wild Bill Hickok, and the more prosaically named Al Sieber, Amos Chapman, Billy Dixon, and Ben Clark.

Cody was twenty-two when he earned the confidence of General Philip Sheridan. A hero of the Civil War next in the public mind only to Grant and Sherman, Sheridan became the instrument of the great national effort to conquer the West. Sheridan's patronage was the most potent and important endorsement Cody would garner. In September 1868, when he carried dispatches through three hundred miles of enemy territory in fifty-eight hours, Sheridan wrote of him: "Such an exhibition of endurance and courage was more than enough to convince me that his services would be extremely valuable in the campaign, so I retained him at Fort Hays [Kansas] till the battalion of the Fifth Cavalry arrived, and then made him chief of scouts for that regiment."[9] The next day Cody's name was added to the payroll at seventy-five dollars a month, more than five times the pay of an army private. As Cody biographer Don Russell put it, "Never again would Buffalo Bill be so little known."[10]

Cody attracted attention for his ability to read the landscape, to remember landmarks in a countryside that seemed virtually featureless to newcomers, to find water, and to trail Indians. He inspired admiration for his horsemanship, his marksmanship, and his stamina. And he was noticed for his coolness under fire. The Fifth Cavalry's field commander, Major Eugene A. Carr, praised Cody highly in an official report about an eventful patrol, not only remarking upon his trailing skills but noting that he "deserves great credit for his fighting in both engagements, his marksmanship being very conspicuous."[11]

In his first month with the Fifth Cavalry, he was involved in four skirmishes with Indians in eastern Colorado and Nebraska. Then Carr's regiment took part in General Sheridan's campaign in the winter of 1868 and 1869, and Cody was praised for "cheerful service under dispiriting circumstances."[12] In the severe weather he carried dispatches, hunted buffalo, and once aided the wagon master in running supply wagons downhill. In a killing blizzard in southeastern Colorado, he led a relief column across an all but invisible landscape to the lost and starving infantry command of General William Penrose and its scout, Wild Bill Hickok.

During the summer of 1869, Cody was given much of the credit for the Fifth Cavalry victory at Summit Springs in northeastern Colorado, one of the most significant engagements in plains warfare. According to the regimental history, he "guided the Fifth Cavalry to a position whence the regiment was enabled to charge the enemy and win a brilliant victory."[13] Cody was twenty-three.

Shortly after the fight, Cody was introduced to the itinerant temperance lecturer and pulp-novelist E. Z. C. Judson, better known as Ned Buntline, who asked him numerous questions. Buntline then used Cody's alliterative nickname and little other factual material in the resulting dime novel, *Buffalo Bill, the King of Border Men*. Cody and Buntline would not cross paths again for three years, but Buntline's lurid romance engendered the legend that he created both a name and a persona for Buffalo Bill.

The Fifth Cavalry engaged in only two fights during 1870 and 1871. Cody was cited for guiding and gallantry in both. There were numerous other guiding chores and long patrols during this relatively quiet period. Cody led hunting trips and honed his social skills on visiting dignitaries and scientists who could make claims on the army's hospitality. He and Louisa lived at Fort McPherson, Nebraska, where two of their four children were born.

In the fall of 1871 he guided a hunt for General Sheridan and a party of military brass and eastern swells. One of the group, General H. E. Davies, wrote a small book about the excursion, *Ten Days on the Plains*, in which he mentioned Cody often and flatteringly. Frontier scouts, many of whom self-consciously adopted chivalric dress and manners, were noted for their flamboyance. Cody, in fact, practiced a little showmanship on Sheridan's party, dressing colorfully and riding a white horse. "I determined to put on a little style myself," he wrote.[14]

142

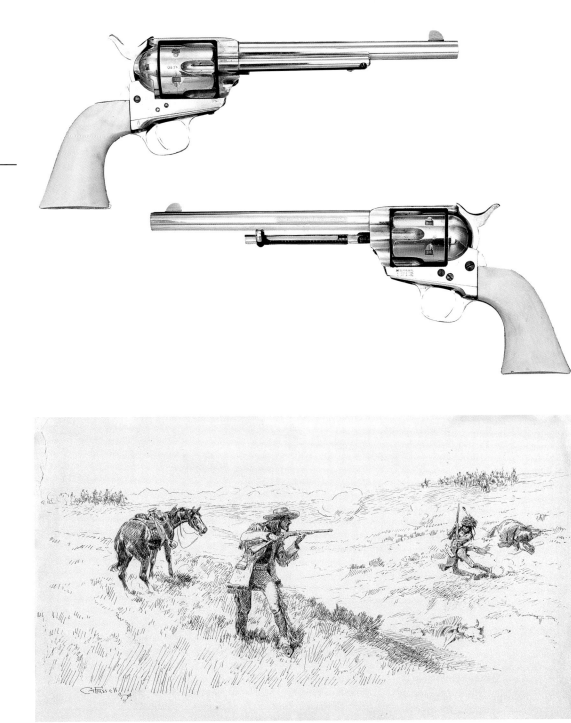

Buffalo Bill's pair of Colt Frontier .44 caliber six-shooters with ivory handles. 1885
Courtesy of the Buffalo Bill Historical Center, Cody, Wyoming.

Charles Russell
Cody's Fight with Yellowhand. c. 1922
Pen and ink, and graphite on paper
14¼ x 22½ in
Amon Carter Museum, Fort Worth.

143

One historian called this expedition a rehearsal for the most famous of all western hunts, the one staged early in 1872 for the Grand Duke Alexis of Russia.[15] Sheridan again named Cody to be guide, this time ordering him to remain at Fort McPherson while the rest of the Fifth Cavalry was transferred to Arizona.

Alexis's visit grabbed the public imagination. Russia was mysterious and vaguely eastern anyway. But the Czar had remained steadfast in friendship with the United States during the 1860s while Britain and France flirted with the Confederacy. At a time when war with Britain seemed possible, Russia's alliance was bolstering. In addition, by 1872 the Russian sale of Alaska to the United States was beginning to reveal itself as the bargain it was. The hunt itself was a grand safari on an operatic scale with two companies of cavalry, the entire village of Sioux Chief Spotted Tail, endless bottles of champagne, and as guides—Cody and Custer. In any case, the visit of Alexis inspired complete press coverage, and Buffalo Bill found himself in headlines for the first time, both in the United States and abroad.[16]

At Sheridan's suggestion, and at the invitation of eastern friends, Cody took a paid leave in March of 1872 to visit Chicago and New York. There, to his astonishment, he saw an actor portraying Buffalo Bill in *The King of Border Men*, adapted from the Buntline novel. He also was treated to lavish hospitality, undoubtedly whetting his appetite for more.

Almost immediately upon his return to Fort McPherson he was plunged into action, this time with the Third Cavalry. On April 26, 1872, he guided a squad of cavalry to within fifty yards—almost point-blank range!—of an encamped Sioux raiding party he had been trailing for a day and a half. Attracting fire, Cody led the charge, killed one Sioux, and recovered several stolen horses. For this he received the Medal of Honor, one of only four civilian scouts during the Indian wars to be so recognized.

By the end of the year the Indians had begun to withdraw from the area and the prospect of further fighting waned. Cody resigned as a scout in December 1872, and with his friend Texas Jack heeded Ned Buntline's call to Chicago to star in *Scouts of the Prairie*. The adulation of their audiences and the relatively easy money lured both Jack and Bill to new careers. A year later they formed their own combination, commissioned their own play, and persuaded Wild Bill Hickok to join them.

The plays made little sense, at first, but what did it matter? They were vehicles for their stars, and the stars were not only living dime-novel heroes, they were the real thing. Cody quickly became a matinee idol. He returned west in 1874 to guide a hunting trip and sign on as chief scout for Colonel Anson Mills's Big Horn Expedition. Then, significantly, he returned to the stage. The only role he attempted to play was himself, Buffalo Bill, and his audiences understood that he actually was what he portrayed on stage. But he also had the indefinable quality we call charisma.[17] Tall, slender, strong, incredibly handsome—men said so as well as women—graceful on horseback, even Mark Twain acknowledged that Cody seemed to be a knight in an age that yearned for chivalric values.[18] With increasing sophistication, Cody's appreciation of the theater and its possibilities grew. So did his artistry, and his fame.

By 1876, the nation was girding itself for the great centennial blowout, and thousands of Sioux were gathering on the Montana plains for what would be a climactic summer in the Indian wars. Meanwhile, with his family settled in Rochester, New York, Cody was a thirty-year-old man of affairs and a retired frontier legend. Events in July would transform him from mere legend into genuine mythic hero.

There were good reasons why Cody should be singled out for fame in both the military and civilian worlds. In the years of demobilization after the Civil War, army strength and morale reached low ebb. Officers were faced with rank stagnation, spending years at junior grades. There was little mobility and precious little glamour. The Indian wars were not headline material: they usually were reported in brief in the eastern press in columns headed "From the Plains" or "Other Communications."[19]

Military men well understood that there was little glory to be won fighting Indians. On the one hand they were supposed to be racially and organizationally superior, and it was expected that they should easily prevail. On the other, their critics and much of the press called them bullies for doing so.

But given the exigencies of plains warfare the army was slow to adjust. Officers were trained for European-style conflict, for the Germanic set-piece battles that characterized the Civil War. Soldiers were garbed and armed with outdated equipment and drilled for anachronistic tactics. The plains wars more closely resembled guerrilla warfare. Individual heroics stood out. Flamboyant fighters like Cody were admired by soldiers because they hearkened back to chivalric values. They were dashing, daring, colorful, and successful. Furthermore, an army unit in the field was frequently utterly dependent on the guide for his knowledge of the terrain, the forage, and the enemy. "He enjoys a brilliant reputation as a scout and guide," wrote the Fifth Cavalry's regimental historian of Cody, "which has been fairly earned by faithful and conspicuous services."[20] The key word is "conspicuous." Not bound by military discipline, Cody and his confreres dressed and acted extravagantly, and their conspicuous heroics reflected glory on their regiments.

In the civilian world there was no less a yearning for heroes and a groping for unity. The Civil War split in the nation was exacerbated rather than healed during the early years of Reconstruction. In the North, the rapid industrialization of the war years continued. The waves of immigrants from Ireland and the continent, interrupted during the war, resumed and filled the factories and cities.

On the eve of the nation's centennial, there were at least three major alienated constituencies in America: northerners, southerners, and immigrants, not to mention Indians and blacks whose voices were heard mainly through the sufferance of white humanitarians.

Greed fueled the economy. In 1873, the year that Mark Twain and Charles Dudley Warner coined the name for the era with their novel *The Gilded Age*, the nation suffered yet another depression brought on in part by speculation and overexpansion. The transcontinental railroads were still collecting vast sections of land in the government giveaway that Vernon Parrington called "The Great Barbecue." "It was an

anarchistic world of strange, capable men, selfish, unenlightened, amoral," he wrote.[21] Grant's administration was permeated by corruption and rocked by scandal.

Yet in the West Americans still saw romance and heroism. It was the place where the national spirit was being healed and renewed. There were heroic engineers such as Grenville Dodge laying out railroads and highways and explorers such as John Wesley Powell who were taming and naming the rivers and canyons. Most important, the West belonged to everybody. It was territory held in common by all the states. The conquest of the West would be a national enterprise in which everyone in America could share, even if only vicariously. Western themes and settings pervaded popular entertainment; and with plays such as *Life on the Border* and *Scouts of the Prairie* being written for him, Buffalo Bill was in the vanguard of what theater historian George O'Dell called "the epidemic of border drama."[22]

At the Centennial Exposition in Philadelphia, in 1876, Americans gathered to celebrate progress, their technological liberation from the past. The undisputed hit of the fair was the gigantic Corliss steam engine, the largest ever built, which powered every other machine in the exposition. "Here is Prometheus unbound," boasted one reporter in a fit of hubris. Alexander Graham Bell's telephone attracted nearly as much attention.[23] Walt Whitman captured the national mood in "To a Locomotive in Winter" when he wrote: "Type of the modern—emblem of motion and power—pulse of the continent,…Law of thyself complete, thine own track firmly holding."[24]

Two summer events in the far-off West, less than a month apart, would successively shatter Centennial smugness then help to redefine, to crystallize the nation's myth of the West. Not coincidentally, they would thrust Cody—who had been asked by Major Carr to rejoin the Fifth Cavalry—back into the public eye as a warrior. First, shockingly, on June 25, 1876 Civil War hero George Armstrong Custer and more than 260 men of the elite Seventh Cavalry were overrun by Indians at the Battle of the Little Big Horn in southeastern Montana. Coming together in outrage, North and South eulogized Custer as a martyr to the conquest of savagery. His death was a mythic sacrifice to national unity; for once all eyes were focused on the West. From this point, the American people promised all necessary tools for conquest.

Then, little over three weeks later, lightning struck at Warbonnet Creek, Nebraska, on the road to the Little Big Horn.

Early in the morning, July 17, seven companies of the Fifth Cavalry, 330 men, had just completed a march of eighty-five miles in thirty-one hours to intercept a band of Cheyenne headed by Beaver Heart, Buffalo Road, Yellow Hair (better known to posterity as Yellow Hand), and their chief, Little Wolf. Little Wolf was taking his people—about four hundred warriors—north from Red Cloud Agency, Nebraska, to join their brothers who had been victorious at the Little Big Horn less than a month before. Emotions were high on both sides.

Before dawn, scout W. F. Cody reported to headquarters, Fifth Cavalry, that he had found the Cheyenne and that their camp was ready to move. Shortly past 4:15 a.m., Company I lookout Corporal Wilkinson pointed southwest toward distant Pine Ridge and said to First Lieutenant Charles King, "Look, Lieutenant, there are the Indians."[25] Lieutenant King positioned trooper Christian Madsen as an advance lookout on a rise overlooking the Cheyenne's probable route. King and Corporal Wilkinson occupied a nearby hill, closer to the main command which ranged behind a low bluff. By 5 a.m., the Cheyenne were closing in leisurely fashion on the cavalry position.

Colonel Wesley Merritt, the regiment's commander, asked "Have the men had coffee?" Then he ordered the troopers to readiness. Meanwhile, scout Cody noticed a small party of Cheyenne leaving the main band and approaching the cavalry position on the run. They intended to catch a pair of army couriers riding unaware towards Merritt's command.

Cody proposed to head off the Cheyenne and rescue the couriers. Merritt assented and allowed Cody to lead the small rescue party. The lookout, Lieutenant King, waited until the critical moment then gave the signal: "Now, lads, in with you!"[26] Cody closed on the Cheyenne leader Yellow Hand. Both men fired. Both horses fell. Cody recovered and shot Yellow Hand, scalped him, and in a gesture of triumph raised the scalp and warbonnet to the cheering men of the regiment as they thundered by. He may have yelled "First scalp for Custer!"[27]

The rest of the Cheyenne scattered, abandoning their gear and provisions, and dashed back to Red Cloud Agency with the cavalry on their tail. There they sat out the rest of the Great Sioux War.

At nearby Fort Robinson, Cody paused to write a hasty and breathless letter to his wife to tell her of the fight. He killed Yellow Hand in front of the regiment, he told her, "and the cheers that went up when he fell was [sic] deafening." Most tellingly, he wrote, "You will no doubt read of it in the papers."[28]

And she did. What is most extraordinary about this story is that it is true. The accounts that appeared in the New York press within the week used highly dramatic language to describe the action, but mortal combat and the clash of cavalries are always sensational events.[29]

This proved to be the climax of Cody's scouting career. It would have climaxed the career of any warrior, white or red, to boast of a victorious single-handed fight. But it was Buffalo Bill, the stage star, who risked all to kill a Cheyenne warrior in that most chivalrous of acts—a single combat to the death, man to man, in front of the whole regiment, and avenging Custer no less. What if John Wayne, after whipping the Japanese on film, had actually led the charge up Mount Suribachi?

The fight was inevitably exaggerated in the retelling, but its effect could hardly be exaggerated. Cody the warrior had validated Cody the actor. Fact and fiction were from that moment conjoined in Buffalo Bill, and his retelling of western history on the stage or in the arena would carry the weight of truth. This splashy but minor skirmish became the most significant event in Cody's career and a turning point in the way the world would come to view the West. Cody's audiences believed him; they accepted his show as "a show of the truth as it was."[30] And the show's narrative carried for most of them the force of myth.

As it became clearly defined in Cody's life and disseminated through his shows, the myth of the West was first of all a myth of accomplishment shared by all Americans, hence a myth of unity. The "winning" of the West embraced many episodes of heroic labor, from the Pony Express to the laying of track to the busting of sod.

It was next a myth of conquest pitting civilization against savagery. Elements of violence and race are part of the makeup, but conquest was not understood in strictly racial terms. The battle was waged against savagery, which was represented by wilderness, by "Lo, the poor Indian," and in fact by a host of nativistic fears. Cody personalized the struggle for civilization in his fight with Yellow Hand. The irony is that he also glorified the hunter and the wanderer in his Wild West shows. He celebrated the reckless freedom of the cowboy, but he also staged the wagon-train migrations and extolled pioneer settlement. As both plainsman and town builder, from his career on the prairie to his development of Cody, Wyoming, he reconciled in his own life the values of civilization with the romantic elements of the wild and so helped preserve the illusion of freedom and the attendant values of rugged individualism in the West.

Finally, it was a myth of progress, of continuous material growth as well as spiritual renewal. The West was the future. Everyone, of whatever race, could have a share in the future by abandoning the old ways and going along with the new majority culture. In fact, in mining, ranching, irrigation projects, hotels, and newspapers, Cody invested his own wealth heavily in this vision of progress, counting on rapid population growth and the exploitation of natural resources.[31]

In his life and in his Wild West shows, Cody provided a narrative structure that made the myth of the West easy to assimilate. General William Tecumseh Sherman wrote to Cody, "You have been modest, graceful, and dignified in all you have done to illustrate the history of civilization on this continent during the past century."[32] Editor William Allen White would write, "The Wild West always has had with it one real genuine bit of the wild west's nature and character embodied in the commanding figure and compelling personality of the chief of all scouts —Buffalo Bill."[33]

Cody's was not an ordinary life. His exploits came to be sensationalized by a press and public that doted on his career for more than forty years. "His West was a place," wrote historian Paul Hutton, "where the lines between reality and myth became hopelessly blurred."[34] It may be true, as some have suggested, that even Cody himself near the end of his life was unable to discriminate between the real and the imputed Buffalo Bills. If so, it is because in the act of vanquishing Yellow Hand at Warbonnet Creek, Cody became more than real; he became part of the myth of the West.

Paul Fees is senior curator at the Buffalo Bill Historical Center in Cody, Wyoming. Author of numerous publications, his scholarly focus has been on the art and culture of the American West.

Buffalo Bill's Wild West. c. 1890

Color lithograph poster

28½ x 22 in

Courtesy of the Buffalo Bill Historical Center, Cody, Wyoming.

• **Unknown**
The White Eagle. c. 1890

Lithograph poster

Courtesy of the Buffalo Bill Historical Center, Cody, Wyoming.

• **Unknown**
Custer's Last Stand as Presented by Buffalo Bill's Wild West. c. 1904

Lithograph poster

Courtesy of the Buffalo Bill Historical Center, Cody, Wyoming.

• **Unknown**
Scenes of Summit Springs Rescue. c. 1907

Lithograph poster

Courtesy of the Buffalo Bill Historical Center, Cody, Wyoming.

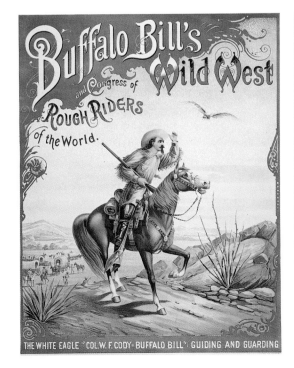

Annie Oakley's gun

Winchester model 1892 carbine, .32 caliber, gold finished, factory engraved with elk scene and initials A. O.

Courtesy of the Buffalo Bill Historical Center, Cody, Wyoming.

Unknown

Buffalo Bill Wild West Show Troop, San Francisco. 1902

Panoramic photograph

Courtesy of the Buffalo Bill Historical Center, Cody, Wyoming.

Stacy Portrait Studio
Untitled (Buffalo Bill). c. 1895
Albumen print
16½ x 13³⁄₁₆ in
R. Joseph and Elaine R. Monsen Collection.
Photo by Richard Nicol.

149

RESTATING THE WEST

Cover of *Artforum* magazine, February, 1990,
with James Caan and John Wayne in
Howard Hawks' *El Dorado*, 1967.
Photo courtesy of Photofest.

ARTFORUM

INTERNATIONAL

FEBRUARY 1990 $7.00

From John Ford's *Cheyenne Autumn*, 1964.
Photo courtesy of the Museum of Modern
Art Film Stills Archive.

The notes for the text begin on page 188.

Graves and Grails: Mythic Landscape in Western Fictions

Kathleen Murphy

"But where is what I started for so long ago?
And why is it yet unfound?"[1]
Walt Whitman, 1860

In the 17th and 18th centuries, those Europeans who stood on the edge of the Old World gazing westward toward America had at their backs noisy, teeming, already polluted cities, leveled forests, and constricted countrysides long ago divvied up among the privileged. Beneath their feet the ground was layers deep with the debris of previous civilizations. Europe's social systems, the very air her populations breathed, seemed clogged and opaque with complexity, centuries-old corruption.

From the perspective of these pilgrims, all of the brave new world of America was the West. But once they had achieved a foothold in the eastern environs of the capacious continent, the West ceased to be either stationary or infinite. Synonymous with wilderness, it always lay just beyond the advancing wave of settlements. The Pacific Ocean eventually put a stop to the land; yet the remarkable dreams—and nightmares—this promised land engendered move us to this day.

America—the West—must have been a welcome tabula rasa to those early newcomers, hot on the trail of second chances. A man could write his own ticket, chart his own course. The clean slate was soon filled with fictions, dramas, and journeys that became the psychic landscape of the West. It is this mythic territory that American writers and filmmakers have mapped, surveying from spiritual, psychological, and existential coigns of vantage. Depending on their bent, these explorers have variously traced out the signatures of Nature, God, Satan, man, and machine in the West's wide, open spaces.

In *A Writer's America: Landscape in Literature*, Alfred Kazin notes that "America's 'sacred places' were made so not by religion but by attachment to places that spelled safety."[2] And, one might add, to places where Something Happened, an event or odyssey that stuck in the collective memory, fattening the myth. In American novels and films, such places have included a brightly lighted town or a new-found promised land, havens from "Nature red in tooth and claw"; a trackless wilderness or a broad river, where noble savages could escape the taint of civilization; a rugged mountain range in which a wanderer might find himself, or one of the masks of God; or just the earth where someone on the way to somewhere was laid to rest.

Significance does not reside in the place, but in the "spelling." From artist to artist, the focus may shift and a zone of safety or redemption may be transformed into a precinct of profound risk—a dark place where men and dreams go bad, and souls, sanity, even lives, are lost. Like Ernest Hemingway's aptly named Big Two-Hearted River, the mythic landscape of the West is always in motion, inviting epic journeys that damn or redeem or, sometimes, simply dead-end.

Steeped in nostalgia and wish-fulfillment, one "spelling" of the West as sacred ground grew out of the primal desire—still strong today—to backtrack to a simpler, more innocent existence in harmony with Nature. Pictured as a borderless garden, unspoiled and naturally fruitful, the western landscape could be read like a primer on how to live ethically: not because society demanded it, but because our deepest natures desired it. No European monuments to the past diminished the new American Adam, though he stood in proper awe of the grandeur of cathedrals, amphitheaters, and fountains worked solely by Nature. In these Edenic landscapes, American writers and filmmakers discovered versions of salvation, secular and divine: such transcendental vistas could only lead the eye toward the visage of God, or, at the least, humankind's best face.

Among the best maps of this American landscape of desire are James Fenimore Cooper's five Leatherstocking novels (*The Pioneers*, 1823; *The Last of the Mohicans*, 1826; *The Prairie*, 1827; *The Pathfinder*, 1840; and *Deerslayer*, 1841). Each features another incarnation of the heroic Natty Bumppo—as Leatherstocking, Pathfinder, Deerslayer, Hawkeye—who sets the pattern for all the strong, silent, and deadly western isolatos to come in American cinema. As D. H. Lawrence points out in his definitive *Studies in Classic American Literature*, Cooper's wish-fulfillment fictions about an unsocialized hunter and his Indian soul mate Chingachgook (close kin to Huckleberry Finn and Nigger Jim) progressively turn back time and drive deeper into "yearning myth": Natty Bumppo regresses from old age to golden youth, while the American wilderness steadily pushes the eastern settlements back toward the sea.[3]

Cooper documents the power of this version of the myth of the West, as well as—by implication—its fatal flaw: Americans dreamed that their virgin land was proof against the inroads of history and progress, that it was endlessly self-renewing. Despite the clear-cutting, the settlements, the slaughter of the buffalo and the Indians' starvation, the wagon trains, the railroads, the mining, and all the other sins of civilization, the land—and the Westerner's innocence—would never wear out.

American writers such as Nathaniel Hawthorne took a darker reading of the American scene, tapping into the possibility that God's Garden, seen in a certain lurid light, might also be the Devil's Playground. Thus, in *The Scarlet Letter*, 1850, Hawthorne's moral cartography traces the connections between Puritan settlement, locus of human law and necessary repression of individual passion, and New England wilderness, promising personal freedom, but also implying the potential for unchecked savagery. For Hester Prynne, Hawthorne's fallen Eve, the forest surrounding the settlement is a mixture of sunlight and shadow where paradise might be regained or lost forever. Similarly, the town's complexion shades from heaven to hell and back again. God may still govern Hawthorne's morally charged terrain, but this writer's grasp of how environment may mirror—ambiguously—the complex landscape of an outcast human soul directly anticipates the great cycle of darkly "psychological" Western films directed by Anthony Mann.

D. H. Lawrence fully appreciated the lure of Fenimore Cooper's fantasy of a western hero, half wild man, half child of God, who found himself, with his Indian brother, utterly at home in the American scene. But in his understanding that the great beckoning vacancy of the West might swallow up all forms of spiritual or secular heroism, triggering an atavistic return to brute existence, Lawrence pointed out that "white men have probably never felt so bitter anywhere as here in America, where the very landscape, in its very beauty, seems a bit devilish and grinning, opposed to us."[4]

From this perspective, the "alien stare" of the Indian projected the intransigent Otherness of America's "unhumanized vastness."[5] The Red Man's physiognomy patterned the landscape of unfettered wilderness: in some sense, he was Nature. For those mythmakers who saw Nature as Bible, the Indian read as a chapter on prelapsarian innocence, and was worthy companion to the American Adam. For those to whom a man the color of blood or night could only be kin to the original Dark Angel, Indians were incarnations of fallen man's barely repressed savagery. Whether the Indian was demon or angel depended on whether the mythic landscape of the West was exempt from or tainted by Original Sin.

The mythic landscapes of America—and the West—are most frequently and powerfully defined in journeys. Whereas Fenimore Cooper, homesick for Eden, propelled his hero back in time in quest of innocence and eternal youth, a far more prevalent journey in American literature and film drove the hero out of youthful idealism into despair, and sometimes death. American critic Leslie Fiedler associates this latter journey with "nostalgia for a time when insanity could be heroically lived out in a landscape indistinguishable from nightmare."[6]

A telling comparison can be made between Natty Bumppo and Nathan Slaughter, the title character of *Nick of the Woods*, 1837, an obscure but provocative novel by Robert Montgomery Bird. A Quaker who settles his family in the wilderness of Kentucky, Slaughter subscribes to living harmoniously with Nature and the noble savage. When the local Indians repay his trust and hospitality by cruelly massacring his family, Nathan Slaughter is transformed into "Old Nick" or "Dead Man Who Walks." The West darkens into hellish relief as this American revenant stalks, executes, and mutilates one Indian after another—eerily foreshadowing Ethan Edwards's quest for revenge in John Ford's film *The Searchers*, 1956.

Nathan Slaughter bears an awful scar on his brow. It is the mark of an American Cain, his hand forever raised in outrage against the empty, indifferent blankness of the American scene, embodied variously in Red Men and a White Whale, weather and terrain, and in the projections of the marked man's own psyche. Always a sign of loss and exile, the scar is the recurring signature of the deeply divided or double natures of many of the heroes, the landscapes, and the myths that figure so largely in fictions about the American West.

American—and more specifically, western—landscapes invited pilgrimages that doubled as journeys into actual wilderness and, less literally, into self and soul. In the tradition of Herman Melville's *Moby Dick*, Mark Twain's *Huckleberry Finn*, and Walt Whitman's peripatetic poetry, Western cinema gravitated toward the rites of passage endured by heroic loners, and sometimes whole communities, as they "threw themselves naked on the hard heart of the country that was calculated to try the endurance of giants."[7] In cinematic and literary fictions, each region of that hard heart—mountains, forests, caves, salt flats, deserts, plains, rivers, and more—posed a unique challenge to the explorer: write large or be erased. The environment was immanent with the power to ennoble or to encourage the slide into primitivism.

When King Arthur's knights quested for adventure and the Holy Grail, or Chaucer's pilgrims set out for Canterbury, the mettle of their very souls was sure to be tested along the way. Fundamentally, however, these travelers were anchored by predetermined roles in their social structure and the familiarity of the terrain. Civilization was a moveable

feast, from town to town, castle to castle. One could never forget oneself, for "the old countries were worn to the shape of human life, made into an investiture, a sort of second body, for man."[8]

In contrast, the western voyager, "detached in measureless oceans of space"[9] and stripped of all the old European signs of selfhood, often had to define himself from the inside out. He might choose to become a kind of existential confidence man, inventing himself as he went along, keeping his identity fluid enough to deal with each new scene. Or he might opt to armor himself in sustaining forms, such as the knightly ritual and Irish-Catholic chivalry of John Ford's western horse-soldiers. Some simply chose to internalize the landscape's Otherness, becoming, according to D. H. Lawrence's definition, white Indians: "These strange, fearless, and adamantine men became almost as inaccessible to passions and wants, and as sufficient unto themselves, as the trees, or the rocks with which they were conversant."[10]

We can glimpse what men of this latter stripe might have looked like in Richard Avedon's remarkable collection of black-and-white portraits, *In the American West*.[11] The eyes and faces and bodies of Avedon's contemporary drifters, dirt-encrusted miners, carnies, slaughterhouse workers, et al., signal that the West has gotten inside and possessed them. They are carriers of its alien wildness, its empty spaces, its very ground and blood.

From the beginning, filmmakers treated the expressive visages of all these western types as just another version of landscape. Through decades of movies directed by masters of the genre (specifically John Ford and Howard Hawks), John Wayne's increasingly Mount Rushmore-like physiognomy almost literally became a cinematic "sacred place" in the mythic West. In *Red River*, the classic 1948 Hawks Western, Wayne's Thomas Dunson turns adamantine during an historic cattle drive through the hard heart of the West. In any film by Howard Hawks, environment figures as a lethal testing ground, a medium that always threatens to wipe out his heroes if they are not sufficiently fast and flexible in adapting to change. The landscape in Hawks's first Western consists mostly of plains backed by low-lying mountains: its very emptiness provokes empire-builder Dunson to wide-ranging entrepreneurial gestures and ultimately to violence.

Dunson gazes at untenanted Texas, claims the land, and fingers his Red River brand into the very dirt to bring it under his name, an extension of himself. He fills the range with the broad red river of his cattle, as though to make the land pulse and move in harmony with his own bloodstream. But in the course of the cattle drive from Texas north to Kansas, Dunson is so beleaguered by forces—manmade and natural—he cannot bend to his will, he hardens into monomania. Ultimately, it is landscape as "measureless ocean" that triggers Dunson's devolution into "rock," an island of isolated selfhood.

Red River's two funerals demonstrate the futility of Dunson's defense. In the first, mountains curve above the grave, their strong horizontal drift repeated in the line of the lower ground. As Dunson intones Everyman's epitaph—"We brought nothing into this world and it is certain we take nothing from it"—smoke from the fire in the foreground billows up, momentarily erasing an upright branding iron, the few mourners, and the cross that marks the grave. Later, a young cowboy, overrun in a cattle stampede, can be identified only by the checkered trousers someone remembers he was wearing. During his burial, as Dunson repeats the same epitaph, the dark shadow of a great cloud passes slowly across the mountain in the background.

Hawksian communities are bonded in their understanding of this hard-hearted country's power to consign them to permanent anonymity. Their members know that they remain upright in the western landscape just so long as will and time allow. The tide of wilderness always breaks through, as it has in Wright Morris's description of a Nebraskan town becoming landscape:

To the east Lone Tree had lengthened like a shadow, but to the west it ended abruptly on the sky. It not merely ended but the sky swept in to invade it, the flood of light and space washing in upon it like a tide. Washing it away, for the square had receded from the blurred fringe of grass and the slats of a fence like fragments of a battered pier. Whatever remained on this edge of town did so at a risk, and a bad one, for only a huddle of old buildings had survived. They faced to the west—a row of old men who had walked to where the sidewalk ended and stood there thinking their thoughts, ignoring the firing squad of light.[12]

For John Ford, unrivaled director of Western masterpieces, the vertical forms of false-front buildings thrown up in the middle of nowhere are brave human signatures. They both echo and defy the buttes and mesas of Monument Valley, the spectacular Utah-Arizona location he used for so many of his films (*Stagecoach*, 1939; *My Darling Clementine*, 1946; *She Wore a Yellow Ribbon*, 1949; *Wagon Master*, 1950; *The Searchers*, 1956; *Cheyenne Autumn*, 1964); it became one of the most

sacred places in American cinema. Ford was morally and emotionally invested in the Victorian clapboard improbably planted on the edge of Monument Valley or the cluster of shacks a cowboy might espy down on a dark plain, an oasis of flickering lights and distant music. For such pilgrims, going "inside" more often than not meant sanctuary, access to civilized amenities and the law.

Even so, Ford shared Hawthorne's understanding that towns could play hell on free spirits; conversely, he also realized that the quintessential western hero, in one of his manifestations, was death-driven, at home only in killing fields. Such a hero is *The Searchers*'s Ethan Edwards (John Wayne), a latter-day incarnation of Nathan Slaughter, "Dead Man Who Walks." Ethan is an isolato from the film's beginning, a man so large and scarcely contained in his bent for violence that human structures (and strictures) are not enough to contain him. Monument Valley is his proper setting, for his psychic inscape has been eroded down to great, empty spaces where his deepest emotions are buried, and the monolithic outcroppings that signal his *idée fixe*.

The impetus for Ethan's decade-long quest is the brutal rape and murder of his brother's wife, the woman he has always loved but could not stay for. It is a Red—the color of blood and passion—Man who, in assaulting Martha and kidnapping (and later "marrying") her daughter, acts out atrocities only dimly imagined in the darkness behind Ethan's brain. Scar, Ethan's Indian doppelgänger, is moved to savagery that cannot be kept down in environs as inimical to any human order as is Monument Valley—"in its very beauty…a bit devilish and grinning, opposed to us." The valley's huge rock formations resemble the rotten teeth of old gods or rough-hewn tombstones marking their ancient graves. A terrible, primeval beauty informs this majestic panorama, but it celebrates nothing to do with civilization.

Ethan cannot be deterred from his path of vengeance; he is, as Ford would have it, as certain as seasons, as inexorable as the turning of the earth. At one point in his search for his blood brother, Ford's anti-hero cooly fires into an Indian's grave, shooting out the corpse's eyes so that, according to tribal lore, the fallen warrior will be forced "to wander forever between the winds"—precisely Ethan Edwards's ultimate fate. Consequently, at the conclusion of quest and film, Ethan cannot follow Ford's celebrants indoors. His tall figure stands transfixed in the dark doorway, the desolate flats and mesas of Monument Valley blazing in the sunlight behind him. Its inhuman spaces have claimed him for good. The door frame encoffins him: man has become landscape.

Within Ford's natural amphitheater, few signs of human life exist: a lone rider, a stagecoach or wagon train, a thin blue line of horse soldiers or painted Indians poised to attack. In such a context, all of his pilgrims—at least those who choose civilization—must be armored in communal forms and formalities, sometimes to the point of destructive inflexibility. Thus, when officers in Ford's beloved U.S. Cavalry gather around a fallen comrade's grave in gallant ritual, they mean to act out forms that stand up to, and separate them from, the vacancy of their environment. Paradoxically, these human rites are sometimes consonant with the alien majesty of the tombstones of the old gods.

Frequently, one of Ford's characters will visit the gravesite of a friend, lover, or spouse to seek guidance or just to check in. In contrast to Ethan Edwards's barbaric purpose at the Indian's resting place, the easy conversation with the gravestone keeps alive the lost soul and the relationship—civilizing death, rescuing the beloved shade from wilderness. And every time Ford's wagon-train or town-raising folk throw down some boards in a clearing so as to step out the complicated patterns of a square dance, they impose human order on a militantly primitive milieu. When a Fordian pilgrimage reaches an end, one way or another the standing stones have been embellished by the names and histories of his very idiosyncratic heroes and heroines, and Monument Valley's primal silence has for a time been filled with human music.

Sam Peckinpah, designated John Ford's illegitimate son in the genealogy of Western filmmakers, always chose wilderness over clearings. But his superannuated outlaws were kept pretty steadily on the move in an ever-diminishing Wild West, so that their stopping-off points never had much time to develop the lasting resonance of a sacred place like Monument Valley. (Toward the end of Peckinpah's cycle of Westerns, Mexico, last refuge of his wild boys of the road, took on a little of that coloration.) However, something like sacramental ground appears in *Ride the High Country*, 1962, the film that first established Peckinpah as a major chronicler of the West. Here, changing terrain functions as Stations of the Cross while a very secular Christ journeys toward an inevitable crucifixion.

The hero's journey begins in a flatland town infected by progress and all the newfangled gimmickry that comes with it. Steve Judd (Joel McCrea), a once-famous, now aging lawman, blunders into the middle of a red-white-and-blue fete and, mistaking the town's festivities for signs of personal welcome and respect, must be shuffled off to the sidelines by a smartly uniformed cop. No palms for this western savior,

but he does scare up a small-time devil: his old partner, Gil Westrum (Randolph Scott), long since fallen from grace and now shilling for a cheap Wild West show. (Peckinpah deliberately cast McCrea and Scott, familiar stars of innumerable horse operas, so that their deeply weathered faces would work as moral touchstones: human countenance as "high country.")

During their subsequent trek up to Coarse Gold, the bleak mining camp where they are to pick up a bank delivery, Judd and Westrum pass from the claustrophobic shallowness of life in narrow streets and small rooms into the natural grandeur of forested mountains and deep blue lakes. The truths Judd still believes are worth standing up for are at home in these places, in this high country.

As they ascend, Westrum chips away at Judd's commitment to personal honor and the law, tempting him to theft just as, in the wilderness, Satan teased Christ toward sin. The outcome of this temptation will affect a young Adam and Eve for whom the partners have become responsible: a boy with a fast gun and the values of a town-bred con artist; and a runaway farm girl who finds herself up for grabs in Coarse Gold's rock-and-gravel wasteland, where the miners have regressed to near-bestiality.

In the high country, halfway between civilization's mean streets and the dens of primitivism, Steve Judd makes his last stand. By doing so, he not only redeems his compromised friend, but also gifts the "children" with another chance at innocence. At film's end, Peckinpah frames the mortally wounded Judd from a radically low angle, identifying him with the mountain range that backs him. As he slants down out of frame, able at last to "enter [his] house justified," Peckinpah's pilgrim joins that earlier anachronism, Natty Bumppo, who passed away in the Rockies, sitting in a rickety chair under the setting sun.

As we've seen, American filmmakers have mined western locales for moral, spiritual, and existential significance. But in the "psychological Western," sacred places become expressionist Rorschachs, signaling the protagonist's descent into partial or full-blown madness. Points of interest along his or her therapeutic pilgrimage, assuming there is one, come out almost literally in the lay of the land.

At the center of the sexually symbolic landscape in Nicholas Ray's one-of-a-kind *Johnny Guitar*, 1953, stands an unusual western hero: a powerful woman whose hand is equally at home with gun or piano keyboard. Vienna (Joan Crawford) has negotiated her past as a prostitute into currency with which to buy a future: a saloon situated in limbo, halfway between town and the mountain lair of outlaws and directly on the route of a promised railroad. Her desert saloon looms up in the swirling dust, its high false front advertising Vienna's arrogance and forward-thinking. But its rear wall is the raw rock of the butte that backs the structure. The casino is like a psychic carapace, the externalization of an ex-whore's shrewd business acumen and hard-won understanding of the power of primitive appetite.

Vienna's space incorporates cave and civilization, the past and the future. But her hardened sexuality taints the saloon. Thus, her elaborately designed business remains empty, penetrated only by an angry wedge of black-clad townsfolk, with the neurotically repressed Emma Small (Mercedes McCambridge) at its head, and the Dancing Kid (Scott Brady) and his outlaw gang. The town's a bastion of hypocrisy and barely contained violence, bent on crushing Vienna because her up-front sexuality and her saloon take in too much ground. (The townsfolk lose out economically if her casino is designated a train station.) On the other hand, her outlaw suitor and his band offer a retrograde existence, ruled by casual appetite for sex or money.

The dialectic at work in *Johnny Guitar* presses toward psychological, economic, and geographical resolution. While her saloon burns to the ground, Vienna dies—symbolically—at the hands of a lynch mob. Both Emma Small and the outlaw whose "dancing" mocks her (and the town's) neurotic impotence are casualties of the final cathartic violence; one represents an excess of civilized restraint, and the other, of natural instinct. At film's end, Vienna and her proper mate, reconciled, descend from the mountain lair, passing through a naturally camouflaged cave-waterfall. This psychologically sacred place takes the curse off Vienna: she has escaped the cold and lonely cave-casino in the desert, where Machine was meant to stand in for Garden.[13] As Johnny Guitar's new Adam and Eve make their final therapeutic breakthrough, there is little doubt that the Spirit of Place in this particular Eden is Sigmund Freud.

Few western landscapes are as psychologically expressive as those that appear in the great cycle of dark Westerns Anthony Mann directed during the fifties. Mann's rugged environs often resemble wastelands out on the edge of some alien world; they are the equivalent of

the psychotic terrain that marks his characters' minds. *Man of the West,* 1958, his last major contribution to the genre, begins in a settled town dominated by a competent lawman and ends with the restoration of civilized order and sanity. But the nightmare spaces between these anchoring points verge on the surreal as the film's protagonist, Link Jones (Gary Cooper), descends deeper into the hell inside his own psyche.

A reformed outlaw with a particularly savage past, Jones has been sent out by his new community to hire a schoolteacher. His path inadvertently crosses that of his old gang, and he is forced to return to the hideout where he lived during his berserker years. The gray, rotting shack huddles in a verdant, almost boggy hollow: the very climate seems corrupt, as though its chemistry might eat away at that which keeps a man upright. When Link enters this wooden cave to confront the old outlaw (Lee J. Cobb) who made him, he begins the necessary journey into the darkness that is still within him.

From this psychic "swamp," Link, his outlaw "father," and the rest of the gang trek up into barren hills which sit in brute witness as he rediscovers a powerful appetite for sadistic violence. To test his renewed allegiance to the old ways, Link is sent off to reconnoiter a bank the gang plans to rob. His destination turns out to be a ghost town, sprawled out like a broken-limbed corpse on a gritty hillside. Here, he shoots it out with his cousin, the self he might have been if he had remained a member of the savage clan. In this sun-scoured terrain, Link begins the exorcism that allows him to lay his ghosts and stake a claim to sanity for the first time in his life.

Back in the mountains, Link's mad progenitor stands silhouetted on a high ridge, flapping like some black devouring demon, the hard heart of that desolate place and his son's malaise. The Man of the West strikes him down, freeing himself to return to civilization, cleansed of his attachment to psychological and literal wilderness.

In Arthur Penn's *Little Big Man,* 1970, Old Lodge Skins, a Cheyenne chief (Chief Dan George), remarks of the puzzling white race: "They do not seem to know where the center of the earth is." He could not know that, in our most deeply rooted myths, the center of the earth had once been ours by birthright, and we had lost it. Cast out, we shaped our fictions into pilgrimages, hoping to map our way home. And the old Cheyenne, casualty of our manifest destiny, certainly could not understand the dream of staking a claim to a new Eden that sustained all of the

Adams and Eves who streamed into the West two hundred and more years ago.

As the wide, open spaces closed down, the protagonists of films about the Wild West's "last days" simply ran out of room and time, and the dream began to pass into memory. Now, at last, the center of the earth is found, but it is not the one quested for in those early days of energy and hope. This sacred place is most concretely visualized toward the end of Sergio Leone's *The Good, the Bad, and the Ugly,* 1966, when the motley pilgrims of the film's title draw down on each other within a dusty arena enclosed by low, crumbling adobe walls. Radiating out from this central killing ground are lines of seemingly endless graves. No longer the landscape of desire, the mythic West has become a place for endings. Every great Western about the shutting down of the frontier and the dream of unlimited second chances finds a symbolic home in Leone's melancholy setting.

Often, in these "twilight" Westerns, Mexico beckons as the last frontier of freedom. But this underbelly of the West has too much history of its own to stand as another Eden. The only sanctuary offered South of the Border is death—of the spirit and of the body. But in *The Wild Bunch,* 1969, Sam Peckinpah's undesirables have nowhere else to "pull back to." Crowded out of homeland and history, these aging badmen drop down into territory ripe with ways to erode the few illusions about themselves they have left. Rather than going gentle into existential oblivion, Peckinpah's Wild Bunch explodes into cataclysmic violence, writing their names in blood. They make their last stand in a hellish environment: an adobe fortress, its aqueduct-like walls barely keeping the hardscrabble desert at bay. The heat and squalor of the place hurt the eyes; a trick of light turns it into an instant ruin. In this crumbling theater-in-the-round, the end of a world plays out in terrible sound and fury: the last outlaw dies bracing a machine gun so that it's defiantly tilted up toward the gods.

During the concluding moments of *The Wild Bunch,* Peckinpah follows in Fenimore Cooper's footsteps by moving his heroes back in time to an Edenic locale. In a reprise of an earlier sequence, the outlaws ride through the rich green shade and golden sunlight of a tree-arched avenue, while smiling villagers wave farewells and toss flowers, as if honoring the passage of knights from a lost court.

Pat Garrett and Billy the Kid, 1973, Peckinpah's most elegiac Western, continues this movement into landscapes of myth and memory. Knowing that they are marked for death, the film's legendary badmen embark on dreamlike walkabouts to find the best time and place to lie down for good. For them, that place cannot be South of the Border; Billy the Kid (Kris Kristofferson) knows that reputation fades away in Mexico, where even a legend can turn into "just another drunken gringo shittin' out chili peppers and waitin' for nothin'."

The prevailing time of day as *Pat Garrett and Billy the Kid* plays out is just before nightfall, the waning hours of the mythic West: bathed in the last rays of the setting sun, an old lawman, gutshot, sits through his dying beside a stream, Bob Dylan's "Knockin' on Heaven's Door" fitting accompaniment to his passing; a grizzled riverman solemnly target-shoots from his raft in the day's dwindling light, and just as solemnly trades friendly fire with Pat Garrett (James Coburn), lounging at his ease under a tree; Billy, barechested after lovemaking, sips a cold beer on a broad veranda, the saturated blue-pink dusk of a balmy southwestern evening covering the approach of his executioner.

While Peckinpah's protagonists are caught in the act of becoming western shades, the main character in Sergio Leone's *Once Upon a Time in the West*, 1969, is almost certainly a revenant, reanimated by the power of memory. Leone transforms the very physiognomy of The Man with the Harmonica (Charles Bronson) into the brown planes and creases of desertscape, his eyes the searing blue of cloudless southwestern skies, and maps this pitiless wilderness in long, mesmerizing close-ups. The Man is the West, leached of hope.

One of those "adamantine men almost as inaccessible to passions and wants as the trees, or the rocks," this mysterious figure has literally become one with landscape, a western haunt. Indeed, at one point, Leone's camera enters The Man's eyes to find the location of the only—the last?—place he seems to have truly lived. Improbably, in this Italian-made film, it is John Ford's Monument Valley, the Western's most sacred ground. That Leone is performing last rites is underscored by the final word on The Man: "People like that have something inside—something to do with death."

Cinematic last rites gravitate toward circular narratives (and images), sometimes to mourn the futility of the journey, sometimes to suggest its formal completion. Few Westerns exploit that itinerary more ambitiously than Simon Wincer's *Lonesome Dove*, 1989, an eight-hour television miniseries adapted from the best-selling novel by Larry McMurtry. Like the American West, *Lonesome Dove*'s landscapes are defined by many overlapping odysseys, the majority of which end in death. This sprawling saga tries to draw in all of the conventions and characters of the Western, every mythic ingredient, as though it meant to house them, once and for all, under one fictional roof.

At the story's outset, a band of semiretired Texas Rangers, about the same age as Peckinpah's Wild Bunch, has washed up on the American side of the Rio Grande, just outside Lonesome Dove, a couple of false fronts fast becoming a ghost town. Stranded on a parched, yellow flat beside the river, these one-time movers and shakers have not yet succumbed to the dubious lure of Mexico—except for an occasional horse-stealing foray.

Out of this apparent cul-de-sac, *Lonesome Dove*'s heroes plunge northward into the heart of the West to seek out a "cattleman's paradise" up in Montana. Their epic drive repeats Fenimore Cooper's fictional itinerary from age to youth, from wasteland to New Eden, and retells the rosary of rivers, towns, forts, badlands, and plains that have become the sacred sites of the West.

As the landscape of Camelot was defined in the perfect bonding of Arthur and Guinevere, the mythic center and movement of *Lonesome Dove* are located in the partnership of Woodrow F. Call and Augustus McCrae. Along with Deerslayer and Chingachgook, Huck Finn and Nigger Jim, Pat Garrett and Billy the Kid, and all the other American doppelgängers, these two express the double nature of the mythic West. Woodrow F. Call, brooding, taciturn, fixed in principle and itinerary, is a man to make laws and found empires, a still point aspiring to manifest destiny. A charming word-spinner who makes any hard-going easier, Augustus McCrae has a sweet tooth for every new experience but stopping. Quicksilver at large, unable or unwilling to contain himself, Gus is the best, most innocent avatar of the mythic Westerner.

In the first movement of *Lonesome Dove*, the northward journey toward renewed youth and hope, McCrae is the eternal knight-errant, drifting off into adventures on ground he is visiting for the second and third times. As primary vehicle for our most cherished dreams of the West, Gus moves through his "last days" bidding farewell to sacred

places. Symbolically, he will come to choose death over immobility, when both legs require amputation because of a festering arrowhead wound. The myth of unending second chances and perpetual motion may turn gangrenous, but it will not be brought down to earth without larger-than-life last rites. "Best thing you can do is ride off from it," advises Gus. "Yesterday's gone. We can't get it back." And yet, in his life and in his death, Augustus McCrae stamps our memories with unalterable images of yesterday's wide, open spaces.

167

The great cattle drive claims the lives of all the old knights, save one. And, in the second, southward movement of the saga, Woodrow F. Call becomes the bearer of legend, trekking all the way back to Texas with his friend's corpse. Like some recalcitrant seed, Augustus McCrae won't take root until he's buried in Clara's Orchard, that cool, green pecan grove beside a sparkling stream, "the place [he] was happiest, a live human being free on the earth."

Clara's Orchard is one of those Edens our European ancestors, poised on the shores of the Atlantic, imagined waiting for them in the fabled West. It is one of the many sacred places of "yearning myth," the American equivalent of Camelot's shining city on the hill. As Arthur is England, so are men like Woodrow F. Call and Augustus McCrae, and all their comrades-in-arms, one with the soil and soul of the dreamed-of West.

Like our myths, Clara's Orchard will always be the locus of paradox. It is the ground in which we plant our most unregenerate innocence in hopes of redemptive fruit, and the place we lay to rest those landscapes of desire that disenchantment has diminished down to grave-size. It comes to that finally: the mythic West has room for multitudes, for God's Garden and the Devil's Playground, for settlers and searchers, for Nature and Machine, for the sweep of land that can swallow a man up without trace but stretches the imagination to its limits, for young men's dreams and old men's memories, and for many, many graves.

The wide, open spaces of the actual West and latter-day Westerns are dominated by things past: cemeteries, ruins, ghost towns. The Chamber of Commerce in Tombstone, Arizona, hawks an annotated map of Boot Hill, where those hard cases who were shot down at the OK Corral lie cheek by jowl with Tombstone's many suicides, and wooden crosses advertise that not even children died naturally here. But each and every one of these western graves, in the landscapes of fiction or history, is a sacred place. Each is a Grail from which flow stories that sustain us.

In *My Antonia*, Willa Cather describes the grave of a man who took his own life under the strain of trying to make a home on the inhospitable prairie:

Long afterward, when the open grazing days were over, and the red grass had been ploughed under and under until it had almost disappeared from the prairie; when all the fields were under fence, and the roads no longer ran about like wild things, but followed the surveyed section-lines, Mr. Shimerda's grave was still there, with a sagging wire fence around it, and an unpainted wooden cross.... The grave, with its tall red grass that was never mowed, was like a little island; and at twilight, under a new moon or the clear evening star, the dusty roads used to look like soft grey rivers flowing past it. I never came upon the place without emotion, and in all that country it was the spot most dear to me. I loved the dim superstition, the dim propitiatory intent, that had put the grave there; and still more I loved the spirit that could not carry out the sentence— the error from the surveyed lines, the clemency of the soft earth roads along which the homecoming wagons rattled after sunset.[14]

Mr. Shimerda's "little island," Clara's Orchard, Natty Bumppo's resting place in the high country, Monument Valley—each is a clean, well-lighted place in the landscape of memory and desire. These are the mythic centers of our American earth, "gone into the whole torrent of years with the souls that pass and never stop."[15]

Kathleen Murphy's film criticism has been published in the *Seattle Weekly, Boston Phoenix, Film Comment*, and *Movietone News*, among others. She is the former program director of the Cinema Studies program at University of Washington Extension.

Chris Bruce

Andy Warhol's *Double Elvis,* 1963, is one of the most succinct encapsulations of the mythic western hero in contemporary art. It is a classic media image, derived from a publicity photo from the 1960 movie *Flaming Star.* Movies are made as entertainment for as large an audience as possible, and their pervasive influence has obviously played an enormous role in popularizing the symbols of the West in the 20th century. Paintings, on the other hand, are generally made for individual contemplation without such attendant publicity. What does it mean when a painting takes a movie image as its source, as *Double Elvis* does?

For one, it means that the artist acknowledges the great distance between historical source and media impression. More to the point, it means the artist himself is part of the audience, recycling already-created images rather than discovering new worlds. In the 19th century, artists went west and returned to the population centers in the East or Europe with rare treasures of visual information. But now, with the same movies and television shows playing world-wide, the audience instantly shares the same well of experience. An artist like Andy Warhol is one of "us," part of the consuming public.

Los Angeles writer Michael Ventura notes that by the 1920s "silent movies had become the experience most Americans had in common—more common, for instance, than their language." He concludes that "Americans are less unified as a people than as an audience."[1] By 1947, seventy-five thousand Americans owned television sets. Less than twenty years later fifty-five million sets had found prominent places in ninety-five percent of the homes in the United States.[2] In those days, Westerns were always part of the package. In 1960, the year *Flaming Star* was made, eight of the top ten rated television shows were Westerns. While film's big screen could be epic in presenting the landscape, the television screen shifted the focus away from CinemaScope panoramas to close-ups, personal dramas, and the confinement of town. This is the media-glazed world *Double Elvis* comes from.

If we look at *Double Elvis* within the historical framework of painting about the West, its most startling characteristic is the general vacuity of descriptive detail beyond the figure, or more specifically, the absence of landscape. Yet the lack of traditional setting gives rise to the realization that the background is, in fact, a very specific context: the movies, the silver screen. Here, rather than merging with some splendid landscape as the romantic figures in the art of the 1800s would have done, Warhol's larger-than-life Elvis is submerged within the glory of 20th-century cinema-scape. The blank silver panel allows us to project our myriad memories of those familiar western details from the back lots of Warner Brothers, Paramount, Universal, and 20th Century Fox. Or we can accept the silver screen as a complete abstract entity unto itself, the symbolic silver ideal in an otherwise cloudy world.

If this is an ideal of sorts, it is one that represents a fundamental split with the larger body of western art, for its only reference to place is to one that is peculiarly beyond nature: Hollywood. The essays in this book have shown how the depiction of landscape increasingly served as the backdrop for the western hero. No longer: in television and movies, the setting is a "set," the landscape is a "location." Irrespective of these studio background painters, the last great painter of the western landscape was undoubtedly Georgia O'Keeffe, and her work is such an anomaly in this century that it is included here primarily as a stunning exception. Interestingly, her work has the formal emblematic quality we associate with artists such as Andy Warhol and Roy Lichtenstein, who set classical, primary images in rarified, abstracted backgrounds. But truly, O'Keeffe's work speaks not about popular culture, but of the sacred purity of the landscape in another world outside of time. She first visited New Mexico in 1917 and returned to visit regularly from 1929 to 1939, when she established permanent residence there. Her work is nothing less than a personal connection to a primal time and place, as though she were the very first human being to bear witness to it.

Andy Warhol. *Double Elvis,* 1963 (detail).
See page 174 and 175.

The notes for the text begin on page 188.

Georgia O'Keeffe
Cow's Skull on Red. 1931-36
Oil on canvas
36x40 in
Museum of Western Art, Denver

170

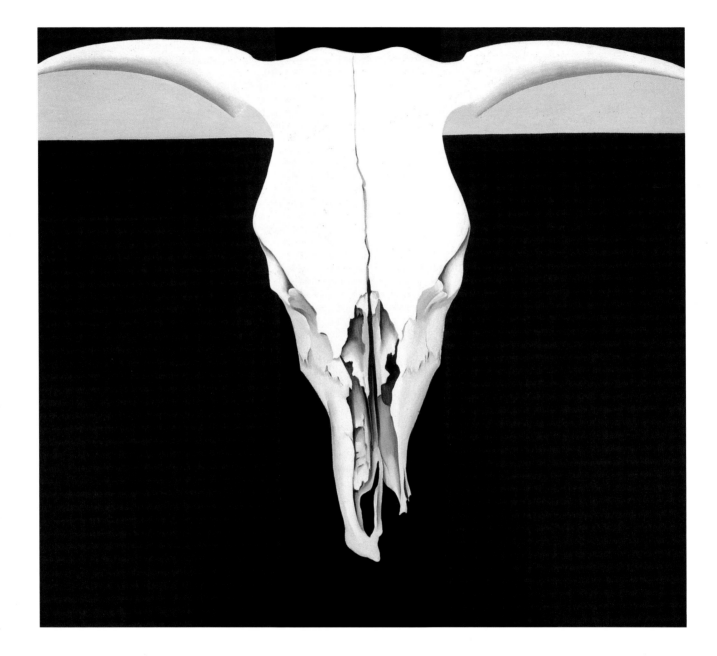

171

Yet for most contemporary artists, the evocative possibilities of landscape are only one side of the double-edged sword that must also include the environmental abuses that have occurred increasingly over the last one hundred years. Painting the landscape as an untainted wilderness today amounts to little more than a nostalgic, romantic gesture. From O'Keeffe's time on, the most serious investigations of the state of the landscape come from photographers like Robert Adams, Lewis Baltz, Richard Misrach, and many others. These artists concentrate not so much on the wonders of the land itself, but on what we have done with it, peeling away ideals and extending our ability to appreciate it as it is, warts and all. Adams has been particularly influential, and he articulated the dilemma in his book *Beauty in Photography* where he says, "Scenic grandeur is today sometimes painful."[3]

This nonromantic view of landscape actually has some precedents as far back as the time of Charles Russell and Frederic Remington, that is, as far back as when the West began to confront its limits, and the audience's interest in figurative dramas replaced descriptions of unknown regions. The 1880s and 1890s were the crucial decades in the development of the fictional western hero, for that time period represents the last gasp of unrestricted movement through the American frontier. From the turn of the century on, the issues in western lore became personal ones of individual freedom battling the more confining aspects of civilization, a prelude to the ecological problems of our own time. What had been an issue of possibility and wide open space became one of restriction, society, settlement, crime, and dreams failed.

It is on this borderland between past and future that the western heroes of 20th-century art have walked, continuing to play out the legacy of Remington and Russell, who portrayed their visions of the terminal Wild West quite deliberately. Both artists were extremely aware of how the West was changing, and knew they were witnessing the end of an era.

Remington said, "I saw men swarming into the land. I knew the wild riders and vacant land were about to vanish forever, and the more I considered the subject the bigger Forever loomed."[4] Similarly, Russell mourned the changes in Montana. Not surprisingly, the conflicting agendas of settlement manifested themselves as the focus of their work, with "scenes constructed around the thunder of horses' hooves, the jammer of profane frontier jargon, and the flow of blood."[5]

For Remington, the landscape was especially utilitarian, an essentially anonymous prop for action. In his *Fight for the Stolen Herd,* 1908-09, the landscape is hardly more than the dust kicked up from the intense action of animal movement and riders in impressive technical control of their mounts and weapons. We see this again in *Fight for the Water Hole,* 1901, which portrays a last-ditch effort to claim a miserable puddle of water—a little blue for the water, a lot of yellow and gray for land. The dispute is clearly futile, for if the attackers don't get them, the water will certainly dry up and they will be forced to move on. Some landscape! But the alternative—to give up—is not pretty, for nobody, especially in the West, likes a quitter. And these paintings do not quit. They freeze the conflict as an emblem of resistance to the impending changes of the 20th century.

Early movies pick up this exact frame of reference, as though a time capsule had been delivered directly from Remington and Russell to such good bad guys as actors William S. Hart and Harry Carey. Director John Ford was especially purposeful in his use of Remington's visualization of the West as a means to infuse his films with a ready-made cultural memory. In a roundabout way, Elvis's pouting rebelliousness is the inheritor of earlier images of defiance, but Warhol goes even further in isolating the man of action from the romantic landscape. And in *Double Elvis,* there is barely the suggestion of a plot, merely this softly reflective reference to cinematic reality.

"In the early 1950s, Nevada was chosen as the site for continental atomic testing because the prevailing wind direction would carry fallout away from the two nearest population centers: Las Vegas and Los Angeles. After the initial tests, however, government scientists made an ominous discovery. The day following the blast known as Simon, on April 25, 1953, clouds in the upper atmosphere transported fallout all the way across the country and dumped it on Troy, New York. This new phenomenon was called the rainout.

"In October and November of 1958, the government rushed to complete its tight testing schedule before the above-ground moratorium went into effect and fired two blasts under unfavorable wind conditions. As a result, low-level fallout drifted into Los Angeles. The facts concerning both these incidents were withheld from the public. Because of concerns over airborne fallout, all testing went underground in 1963. Nonetheless, the American continent continues to be exposed to significant amounts of radiation. To date, there have been eighty-two documented accidents and ventings from underground tests."

Richard Misrach

Richard Misrach
Cloudburst, Nuclear Test Site,
May 1987, Highway 95 Between
Mercury and Las Vegas, Looking
West. 1987
Ektacolor Plus print
40x50 in
Courtesy of the artist and Etherton/Stern Gallery,
Tucson, Arizona.

173

Andy Warhol
Double Elvis. **1963**
**Acrylic and silkscreen on canvas
(silkscreened photographic image)
Each panel: 82¼ x 59⅛ in**
Seattle Art Museum, purchased with funds from the
NEA, PONCHO, and the Seattle Art Museum Guild.

174

Norman Rockwell
Gary Cooper as the Texan. 1930
Oil on canvas
35x26 in
Museum of Western Art, Denver.

This breakdown of narrative in *Double Elvis* is especially evident when comparing it with the central figure in Remington's *Fight for the Waterhole*. Both paintings depict characters who are clearly ready to lay it all on the line to defend their own turf. But there is an important difference. Remington's rifleman points his weapon just off-center, and he looks the other way, beyond the viewer, to his attackers. Remington lets us enter the scene at close range, and lets us know that within the picture frame there is a story being played out. But Warhol's Elvis is a purely confrontational figure who aims his gun directly at us. It is as much an image of survival as the Remington, but in this case the audience is the intruder to be kept on the outside. The image conveys an isolated state of being, not an episode. There is no more narrative here than there is in a stop sign. Elvis keeps the eager, visceral adoration of his fans at bay with a defiant threat of violence and stands as a mute icon to the lonely state of his own fame.

Ironically, while this portrayal of Elvis distances the viewer from the figure contained in the picture, the painting is derived from a publicity still originally used to promote the film *Flaming Star* in 1960. Warhol's painting was produced during the peak of the golden age of Madison Avenue and has the instant recognizability of a billboard. Ultimately, *Double Elvis* presents, *circa* 1963, one terrific package for public consumption, combining the Western movie and Elvis, two of the most popular phenomena of the time. In his absorption of images from popular culture, Warhol was one of the first artists to so completely accept his role in the great American audience. He revels in secondary material as his sources. Then he switches from consumer to producer, never forgetting his roots in the audience. *Double Elvis* is, in fact, one of a number of full-size "products" Warhol made in 1962 and 1963 utilizing this same image: sometimes triple Elvis, sometimes overlapping, sometimes separate as we have here.

Charles C. Cristadero
William S. Hart. 1917; cast 1925
Bronze
37⅜ x 13 x 19 in
University Gallery Collection, University of
Delaware, Newark, Gift of the Gorham Company.
Photo by B. Hulett; Selective Images.

In each one, the black, silkscreened image of our hero appears to dissolve into the silver panel. Silver is also the color of steel, and machines. Warhol said himself, "The reason I'm painting this way is that I want to be a machine."[6] The painting's surface is thin, and this mechanical transparency, along with its reflective background and confrontational gesture, keeps us from responding to this work as a traditional illusionary painting. It functions more as a flat sculptural object, impossible to penetrate.

For comparison, Norman Rockwell's *Gary Cooper as the Texan,* 1930, is another picture of a famous actor by an artist who loved popular culture. It adopts a completely different tactic, one that invites the viewer to consider the fully elaborated details of costume, expression, and situation, as well as the skillful technique of the painter. It is painted in color. The viewer is allowed into the frame to observe Cooper getting ready for his role. We peek through the dressing room window, anticipate the performance, and are curious about it. Rockwell gives us that private behind-the-scenes moment, and like the painters of the previous century, he presents us with something we wouldn't know otherwise. Yet with a different Gary Cooper image, the Solidarity poster, which is Warhol-like in its cool, essential singularity, as well as its mechanical production method, we are given just the public image, the symbol without the storyline. It illustrates the fact that the western hero stands as a mythic figure, able to cross cultural and language borders, to serve as a potent symbol of political action. The poster is hardly a call to consider the specific narrative of *High Noon,* the 1952 film Cooper starred in, even though it is a frame right out of the movie itself. Knowing the film certainly adds an association, but the purpose of the image is something very different, more like a commercial message that brings in the celebrity to make the cause more credible. It triggers a response similar to that of an army recruiting poster shouting "I Want *You,*" and that is what matters.

Roy Lichtenstein's *Fastest Gun,* 1963, and Richard Prince's *Cowboy Series,* 1986-87, extend Warhol's embrace of the familiar emblems of popular culture. These works are further evidence that our love of the West is alive, even if its story is not exactly intact. These pictures also demonstrate the principal characteristic the West seems to connote for the media: timelessness. Here the western images are used to evoke romantic ideals of self-reliance and freedom but, oddly, not specific historical fact or narrative. *Fastest Gun,* made soon after *Double Elvis,* is an image of intimate familiarity perpetuated by its use in just about every Western since the silent era. Lichtenstein painted a number of gun-related works in the mid-1960s, a period of time that immediately followed JFK's assassination in Dallas and Jack Ruby's shooting of Lee Harvey Oswald on national television. Thus, as a simple picture of a handgun, this painting could easily have gotten locked into this highly charged period in contemporary history. It has extended beyond its own moment in time partly because of its comic book style, but also because it calls on the timelessness of the western myth. The same goes for *Double Elvis:* if Warhol had done "the King" in glitter, for instance, it would have dated Elvis utterly, denying the timeless quality given by the western motif.

Advertising prizes imagery that is both iconic and timeless, and no single image has proved as durable as that of the Marlboro Man. He is recognized all over the world, hardly having changed since his inception in 1954 (even though portrayed by innumerable actors). His success as a sales tool is based on the fact that the image, derived from the western myth, is neither past nor present. This sets up a general atmosphere of illusion that allows us to associate the cigarette with men of action and fresh, open air.

Here, the 1980s media-derived work of Richard Prince picks up where Warhol left off. In his elegant, clever photographs, Prince simply rephotographs existing media images and excludes the advertising copy—in this case, the very ads that evoke the western scenes we learned to love in the movies. He does not paint or silkscreen, but instead turns common photographic ad images into fine art photographs. These works are enigmatic: Are they past or present? Fiction or history? In Prince's own words, "They look like they have no history to them—like they showed up all at once."[7] He implicitly demonstrates our uncritical incorporation of the media image into our daily lives where we often treat the flat ad as another reality. He also underscores our disjunction from heritage, for while we in the contemporary world live within galaxies of western images, we rarely see ourselves as part of the story, let alone part of history, as might have been the case a century ago.

Such artists hold up the details of our media-based illusions and unconscious ideals to specific scrutiny. The process of analysis and selection that the work of Prince and others represents is part of a more general inclination by social historians to scratch the surface of western assumptions and images. And yet to say that these particular artists are out to "demythify" the West is to miss the main point, for their work is not satirical, nor is it revisionary. Their work is editorial, identifying and highlighting the key forms of the myth. How information is processed and translated is as pertinent to them as the information itself. They act as professional observers, and yet their lack of bias in viewing the culture does have ramifications, for it inevitably simplifies and fragments whatever is observed, and ignores debate.

Double Elvis, Fastest Gun, and *Cowboy Series* are standards of *contemporary* western imagery because they address our predilection for snippets of information. The essential western images that remain are more symbolic than romantic or descriptive. They call on associations not histories, recognition not contemplation. Yet oddly enough, the most current work here, that of Prince, also turns our attention to whoever these pictured cowboys are, for *someone* was surely out there making the original ads. Weren't they? This could suggest that we have come full circle, that the questions we have asked

about the acceptance of image and media tilt over to a renewed curiosity about the factual and historical reality behind the image. Or, more realistically, just as advertising has learned from art, so artists have learned from advertising, and another layer of fiction has been added to the myth. Richard Prince says, "Advertising images aren't associated with an author. It's as if their presence were complete—classical in fact. They are too good to be true. They look like what art always wants to look like."[8]

As we have seen throughout this book, artists have always looked not so much for historic fact, but for subject matter that stimulates compelling pictures which represent their time. Today, the media offer the visual dramas we share most commonly as a sort of universal vernacular, continuing to expand upon the already wide pool of western imagery from which we draw visions of ourselves.

Artists in Exhibition

Ansel Adams
b. 1902, Carmel, California
d. 1984, Carmel, California

Robert Adams
b. 1937, Orange, New Jersey

Thomas Ayres
b. 1820?, New Jersey
d. 1858, at sea off San Francisco

Lewis Baltz
b. 1945, Newport Beach, California

William Bell
b. 1830, Liverpool, England
d. 1910, Philadelphia

Albert Bierstadt
b. 1830, Dusseldorf, Germany
d. 1902, New York

Karl Bodmer
b. 1809, Riesbach, Switzerland
d. 1893, Barbizon, France

George Brewerton
b. 1827, Newport, Rhode Island
d. 1901, Fordham, New York

Gordon Bushaw
b. 1947, Colfax, Washington

Paul Caponigro
b. 1932, Boston

George Catlin
b. 1796, Wilkes Barr, Pennsylvania
d. 1872, Jersey City, New Jersey

Linda Conner
b. 1944, New York

Charles C. Cristadero
b. 1881, New York
d. 1967, Glendora, California

Rick Dingus
b. 1951, Appleton City, Wisconsin

Laura Gilpin
b. 1891, Colorado Springs, Colorado
d. 1979, Santa Fe, New Mexico

Frank Gohlke
b. 1942, Wichita Falls, Texas

Alexander Hogue
b. 1898, Memphis, Missouri

Harry Jackson
b. 1924, Chicago

William Henry Jackson
b. 1843, Keesville, New York
d. 1942, New York

Len Jenshel
b. 1949, Brooklyn

Frank Tenney Johnson
b. 1874, Big Grove, Iowa
d. 1939, Alhambra, California

Mark Klett
b. 1952, Albany, New York

Roy Lichtenstein
b. 1923, New York

Alfred Jacob Miller
b. 1810, Baltimore
d. 1874, Baltimore

Richard Misrach
b. 1949, Los Angeles

Thomas Moran
b. 1837, Bolton, England
d. 1926, Santa Barbara, California

Georgia O'Keeffe
b. 1887, Sun Prairie, Wisconsin
d. 1986, Santa Fe, New Mexico

Timothy O'Sullivan
b. 1840?, Ireland
d. 1882, Staten Island, New York

Edgar S. Paxson
b. 1852, East Hamborg, New York
d. 1919, Missoula, Montana

Eliot Porter
b. 1901, Winnetka, Illinois

Richard Prince
b. 1949, Panama Canal Zone

Frederic Remington
b. 1861, Canton, New York
d. 1909, Ridgefield, Connecticut

Norman Rockwell
b. 1894, New York
d. 1978, Stockbridge, Massachusetts

Andrew Russell
b. 1830
d. 1902 in the U.S.

Charles Russell
b. 1864, St. Louis
d. 1926, St. Louis

Olaf Seltzer
b. 1877, Copenhagen, Denmark
d. 1957, Great Falls, Montana

John Mix Stanley
b. 1814, Canandaigua, New York
d. 1872, Detroit

Joel Sternfeld
b. 1944, New York

John Vachon
b. 1914, St. Paul, Minnesota
d. 1975, New York

JoAnn Verburg
b. 1950, Summit, New Jersey

Andy Warhol
b. 1928, Pittsburgh
d. 1987, New York

Carleton Watkins
b. 1829, Oneonta, New York
d. 1916, Imola, California

Edward Weston
b. 1886, Highland Park, Illinois
d. 1958, Carmel, California

Richard Prince
Cowboy Series. c. 1980s
Ektacolor print
29½ x 45 in
R. Joseph and Elaine R. Monsen Collection.
Photo by Richard Nicol.

Notes to the Essays

The Myth of the West

1. David Thomson, *Warren Beatty and Desert Eyes* (New York: Vintage Books, 1987), 87.

2. John Szarkowski, *The Photographer's Eye* (New York: The Museum of Modern Art, 1966), 6.

3. Michael Ventura, *Shadow Dancing in the U.S.A.* (Los Angeles: Jeremy P. Thatcher, 1985), 176.

4. Robert C. Cumbow, *Once Upon a Time: The Films of Sergio Leone* (Metuchen, New Jersey, and London: The Scarecrow Press, 1987), 80.

5. Joseph Campbell, *The Power of Myth* (New York: Doubleday, 1988), 15.

6. William W. Savage, Jr., *The Cowboy Hero: His Image in American History and Culture* (Norman, Oklahoma: University of Oklahoma Press, 1979), 88.

7. Lance Morrow, "Charging Up Capitol Hill: How Oliver North Captured the Imagination of America," *Time* 20 July 1987: 12-15.

8. David Halberstam, *The Summer of '49* (New York: William Morrow and Company, 1989), 279.

9. John C. Ewers, ed., *Adventures of Zenas Leonard, Fur Trader* (Norman, Oklahoma: University of Oklahoma Press, 1959), 79-90.

10. Robert G. Athearn, *The Mythic West in Twentieth-Century America* (Lawrence, Kansas: University Press of Kansas, 1986), 63.

Reports from the Field

1. William W. Savage, Jr., *The Cowboy Hero: His Image in American History and Culture* (Norman, Oklahoma: University of Oklahoma Press, 1979), 61.

2. George Catlin, *Letters and Notes on the Manners, Customs, and Condition of the North American Indians*, vol. 1 (1841; reprint Minneapolis, Minnesota: Ross & Haines, Inc., 1965), 21.

3. Catlin, *Letters*, vol. 1, 189.

4. The story of Little Bear and the Dog is based on Catlin, *Letters*, vol. 2, 190-194.

5. Catlin, *Letters*, vol. 2, 193.

6. Ron Tyler, ed., *Alfred Jacob Miller: Artist on the Oregon Trail* (Fort Worth, Texas: Amon Carter Museum, 1982), 34.

7. Bernard DeVoto, ed., *The Journals of Lewis and Clark* (Boston: Houghton Mifflin Company, 1953), lii.

8. Joseph Campbell, *The Hero with a Thousand Faces* (Princeton, New Jersey: Princeton University Press, 1968), 8.

9. Robert G. Athearn, *The Mythic West in Twentieth-Century America* (Lawrence, Kansas: University Press of Kansas, 1986), 273.

10. Catlin, *Letters*, vol. 2, 64.

11. Henry Nash Smith, *Virgin Land: The American West as Symbol and Myth* (Cambridge, Massachusetts: Harvard University Press, 1950), 15.

12. Bil Gilbert, *The Trailblazers* (Alexandria, Virginia: Time-Life Books, 1973), 73.

13. Joslyn Art Museum, *Karl Bodmer's America*, Introduction by William H. Goetzmann, annotations by David C. Hunt and Marsha Gallagher, biography by William J. Orr (Lincoln, Nebraska: Joslyn Art Museum and University of Nebraska Press, 1984), 6.

14. *Karl Bodmer's America*, 11.

15. *Karl Bodmer's America*, 357.

16. Tyler, *Alfred Jacob Miller*, 19. The story of Miller and Stewart is based on Tyler, pp. 19-45. See also Marvin C. Ross, ed., *The West of Alfred Jacob Miller* rev. ed. (Norman, Oklahoma: University of Oklahoma Press, 1968).

17. Tyler, *Alfred Jacob Miller*, 21, 24.

18. Tyler, *Alfred Jacob Miller*, 29.

19. Smith, *Virgin Land*, 89-90.

20. Tyler, *Alfred Jacob Miller*, 51.

21. Tyler, *Alfred Jacob Miller*, 34.

22. Tyler, *Alfred Jacob Miller*, 63.

23. William H. Truettner, *A Study of Catlin's Indian Gallery* (Washington, D.C.: Smithsonian Institution Press, 1979, in cooperation with the Amon Carter Museum of Western Art, Fort Worth, and the National Collection of Fine Arts, Smithsonian Institution), 31.

24. Catlin, *Letters*, vol. 1, 35.

25. Catlin, *Letters*, vol. 2, 3.

26. Catlin, *Letters*, vol. 1, 61.

27. Catlin, *Letters*, vol. 2, 255.

28. Catlin, *Letters*, vol. 2, 249-251.

29. Catlin, *Letters*, vol. 2, 256.

30. Umberto Eco, *The Name of the Rose* (San Diego, California: Harcourt Brace Jovanovich, Inc., 1983), 40.

Bierstadt

1. Gordon Hendricks, *Albert Bierstadt: A Painter of the American West* (New York: Harry N. Abrams, Inc., 1974), 113.

2. Fitz Hugh Ludlow, *The Heart of the Continent* (New York: Hurd and Houghton, 1871), 7.

3. Ludlow, *Heart*, 42.

4. Ludlow, *Heart*, 121.

5. Ludlow, *Heart*, 21.

6. Ludlow, *Heart*, 426.

7. Ludlow, *Heart*, 434.

8. Ludlow, *Heart*, 57.

9. Brucia Witthoft, "The History of James Smillie's Engraving After Albert Bierstadt's *The Rocky Mountains*," *The American Art Journal*, vol. 19, no. 2 (New York: Kennedy Galleries, Inc., 1987): 41-47.

10. Hendricks, *Albert Bierstadt*, 147.

11. Ludlow, *Heart*, 206.

Homage to William Bell

1. Sandy Hume, Ellen Manchester, and Gary Metz, *The Great West, Real/Ideal* (Boulder, Colorado: University of Colorado Press, 1977), 46.

2. John Wesley Powell, *The Exploration of the Colorado River and Its Canyons* (New York: Dover Publications, 1961), 285.

3. Public Law 88-577, U.S. Statutes at Large, 88th Congress, 2nd session, 1964, vol. 78: 891.

4. Roderick Nash, *Wilderness and the American Mind* (New Haven, Connecticut: Yale University Press, 1973), 263.

Remington's West

1. William A. Coffin, "American Illustrations of Today (Third Paper)," *Scribner's Monthly* 11 (March 1892): 348.

2. Julian Ralph, "Frederic Remington," *Harper's Weekly* 17 (January 1891): 43.

3. Perriton Maxwell, "Frederic Remington —Most Typical of American Artists," *Pearson's Magazine* 18 (October 1907): 396, 399, 407.

4. Peggy Samuels and Harold Samuels, *Frederic Remington: A Biography* (Garden City: Doubleday & Company, 1982), 392.

5. On Remington, see Peter Hassrick, *Frederic Remington: Paintings, Drawings, and Sculpture in the Amon Carter Museum and the Sid W. Richardson Foundation Collections* (New York: Harry N. Abrams, in association with the Amon Carter Museum of Western Art, Fort Worth, 1973), and Samuels and Samuels, *Frederic Remington*. For the most recent consideration of his artistry, see Michael Edward Shapiro, Peter H. Hassrick, et al., *Frederic Remington: The Masterworks* (New York: Harry N. Abrams, for the St. Louis Art Museum in conjunction with the Buffalo Bill Historical Center, Cody, 1988); for a "Bibliographic Check List of Remingtoniana," Harold McCracken, *Frederic Remington: Artist of the Old West* (Philadelphia: J. B. Lippincott, 1947), 123-155, the most valuable part of what is otherwise mainly a contribution to the Remington legend; and for a recent collection of his letters, Allen P. Splete and Marilyn D. Splete, eds., *Frederic Remington—Selected Letters* (New York: Abbeville Press, 1988).

6. Orison Swett Marden, *Little Visits with Great Americans; or, Success Ideals and How to Attain Them*, vol. 1 (New York: The Success Company, 1905), 328, 332.

7. Maxwell, "Frederic Remington—Most Typical of American Artists," 403.

8. Coffin, "American Illustrations of Today," 348.

9. Owen Wister, "Concerning the Contents," *Drawings by Frederic Remington* (New York: R. H. Russell, 1897).

10. Owen Wister, "Introduction," *Done in the Open: Drawings by Frederic Remington* (New York: P. F. Collier & Sons, 1903).

11. *Harper's Weekly*, 10 January 1891: 23.

12. *Woman's Home Companion* 30 (June 1903): 38.

13. Frederic Remington to Eva Remington, 22 June 1888, Frederic Remington Papers, Remington Art Memorial, Ogdensburg, New York (Archives of American Art, roll NOR I).

14. Frederic Remington to Owen Wister, undated, in N. Orwin Rush, *The Diversions of a Westerner* (Amarillo, Texas: The South Pass Press, 1979), 137.

15. Frederic Remington to Eva Remington, ca. 18 November 1900, in Hassrick, *Frederic Remington*, 39.

16. Frederic Remington diary entry, in Harold McCracken, ed., *A Catalogue of the Frederic Remington Memorial Collection* (New York: The Knoedler Galleries for the Remington Art Memorial, Ogdensburg, N.Y., 1954), 31.

17. Frederic Remington to Albert S. Brolley, 8 December [1909], Buffalo Bill Historical Center, Cody, Wyoming.

18. Maxwell, "Frederic Remington—Most Typical of American Artists," 399.

19. Similar Remington adaptations include *In a Canon of the Coeur d'Alene* (Century Magazine, June 1888) and *The Bell Mare*, 1907; *A Texan Pony* (Century Magazine, January 1889) and *The Waterhole*, ca. 1907-1908; and *Big Fishing—Indians Hauling Nets on Lake Nepigon* (Harper's Weekly, 4 April 1891) and *Hauling in the Gill Net*, 1909. Sometimes the story might be retained but the composition altered for greater visual impact: *The Apaches Are Coming!* (Harper's Weekly, 30 January 1886) and *The Apaches!*, 1904, for example, and *The Charge on the Sun-Pole* (Century Magazine, March 1890) and *Ceremony of the Scalps*, 1908, destroyed by the artist. The indoor drama of *A Quarrel Over Cards—A Sketch from a New Mexican Ranch* (Harper's Weekly, 23 April 1887) was transformed into an outdoor drama in *The Quarrel*, ca. 1907-1908. Sometimes Remington reworked old material to new ends, integrating figures and poses into entirely different situations. The racing rider in *The Governor's Equipage* (Century Magazine, December 1890) anticipates stalwart Remington cowboys in *Against the Sunset*, 1906, and *Stampeded*, 1908. The Indians congregated *In the Betting Ring* (Century Magazine, July 1889) are gathered to a different purpose in *The Pioneers* (Collier's, 13 February 1904), while the prisoner in *The Shot-gun Messenger* (Harper's Monthly, October 1894) returns as an Indian captive in *Missing*, 1899. The black *Troopers Singing the Indian Medicine Song* (Harper's Weekly, 6 December 1890) become the Indians themselves in *Apache Medicine Song*, 1908, while only the rhythms linking the riders in *The Indian Game of Polo* (Harper's Weekly, 1 August 1891) remain to connect them to the ambitious tableau of riders in *Indian Warfare*, 1908.

20. Edwin Wildman, "Frederic Remington, the Man," Outing 41 (March 1903): 715.

21. Royal Cortissoz, "Frederic Remington: A Painter of American Life," *Scribner's Monthly* 47 (February 1910): 194.

Buffalo Bill

22. Frederic Remington to Owen Wister, September 1902, in Ben Merchant Vorpahl, *My Dear Wister: The Frederic Remington-Owen Wister Letters* (Palo Alto, California: American West Publishing Company, 1972), 310.

23. For the Schreyvogel affair, see James D. Horan, *The Life and Art of Charles Schreyvogel: Painter-Historian of the Indian-Fighting Army of the American West* (New York: Crown Publishers, 1969), 31-40.

24. Samuels and Samuels, *Frederic Remington,* 94.

25. Augustus Thomas, "Recollections of Frederic Remington," *Century Magazine* 86 (July 1913): 354.

26. Leonard Wood, "The Man We Knew," *Collier's* 8 (January 1910): 12.

1. Emerson Hough, "Texas Transformed," *Putnam's Magazine*, 7 (1909-1910): 200.

2. *Anderson Daily News*, Indiana, 24 August 1896.

3. "Buffalo Bill Returns to Shoreline Haunts," *New Haven Register*, 18 May 1989.

4. Thomas Albright, "Buffalo Bill and the Wild West," *San Francisco Chronicle*, 3 July 1983.

5. Malcolm J. Rohrbough, quoted in *The Wall Street Journal*, 22 February 1989.

6. Bernard DeVoto, *The Year of Decision: 1846* (Boston: Little, Brown and Company, 1943).

7. Paul Fees, "The Flamboyant Fraternity," *The Gilcrease Magazine of American History and Art,* 6 (January 1984): i, 1-8.

8. Don Russell, *The Lives and Legends of Buffalo Bill* (Norman: University of Oklahoma Press, 1960), 89-94. Russell's biography is the most thoroughly researched and reliable record of most of Cody's life, particularly of his years as a plainsman.

9. Philip H. Sheridan, *Personal Memoirs of P. H. Sheridan*, vol. 2 (New York: Charles L. Webster and Company, 1888), 301.

10. Russell, *Lives and Legends*, 104.

11. Russell, *Lives and Legends*, 123.

12. Capt. George F. Price, comp., *Across the Continent with the Fifth Cavalry* (New York: D. Van Nostrand, 1883), 584.

13. Price, *Across the Continent*, 135-139, 585.

14. William F. Cody, *The Life of Hon. William F. Cody Known as Buffalo Bill* (Hartford: Frank E. Bliss, 1879), 282.

15. Paul Andrew Hutton, "Introduction," *Ten Days on the Plains* by Henry E. Davies (1871; reprint, Dallas: The DeGolyer Library and Southern Methodist University Press, 1985), 19.

16. There have been numerous published accounts of the hunt, including Cody's own. The newspaper accounts were compiled by William W. Tucker anonymously in *The Grand Duke Alexis in the United States of America* (Cambridge, Mass.: The Riverside Press, 1872).

17. Fees, "Flamboyant Fraternity," 6.

18. Samuel Clemens, "A Horse's Tale," *Harper's Monthly*, 112 (August-September 1906): 328.

19. The best discussion of the frontier army in the post-Civil War years is Robert M. Utley, *Frontier Regulars* (New York: Macmillan, 1973).

20. Price, *Across the Continent*, 585.

21. Vernon L. Parrington, *Main Currents in American Thought*, vol. 3 (New York: Harcourt, Brace, and Company, 1930), 17.

22. George O'Dell, *Annals of the New York Stage*, vol. 9 (New York: Columbia University Press, 1937), 501.

23. Lynne V. Cheney, "1876: The Eagle Screams," *American Heritage*, 25 (April 1974): 32.

24. Walt Whitman, "To a Locomotive in Winter," 1876, reprinted in Sculley Bradley et al., eds., *The American Tradition in Literature*, 4th ed. (New York: Grosset and Dunlap, 1979), 54.

25. A thorough retelling and analysis of the episode, including a compilation of eyewitness narrative, is in Paul Hedren, *First Scalp for Custer: The Skirmish at Warbonnet Creek, Nebraska, July 17, 1876* (Glendale, California: Arthur H. Clark Company, 1980).

26. Russell, *Lives and Legends*, 223-231.

27. Cody, *Life of Cody*, 344.

28. W. F. Cody to Louisa M. Cody, Red Cloud Agency, 18 July 1876 (Cody, Wyoming: Archives, Buffalo Bill Historical Center, MS6, Series I:B, 1/5).

29. E.g., *New York Herald*, 23 July 1876. The *Herald*'s story was based in part on a dispatch written by Lt. Charles King.

30. *Chicago Evening Post*, n.d. 1911 (Cody, Wyoming: comp. in Cody *Scrapbooks*, Archives, Buffalo Bill Historical Center, MS6, Series IX, 20).

31. See, e.g., *Pahaska Tepee: Buffalo Bill's old hunting lodge and hotel, a history, 1901-1946* by W. Hudson Kensel (Cody, Wyoming: Buffalo Bill Historical Center, 1987) for an analysis of Buffalo Bill's extravagant investments in the Cody, Wyoming, region before 1905.

32. Quoted in *Programme*, Buffalo Bill's Wild West, Chicago, 1893 (Cody, Wyoming: Archives, Buffalo Bill Historical Center, MS6, Series 6:A, 1/10).

33. *Emporia Gazette*, Kansas, 1 September 1911.

34. Hutton, "Introduction," 49.

Graves and Grails

1. Walt Whitman, "Facing West from California Shores," 1860, reprinted in Bradley, Beatty, Long, eds., *The American Tradition in Literature,* 3rd ed. (New York: Grosset and Dunlap, 1967), 153.

2. Alfred Kazin, *A Writer's America: Landscape in Literature* (New York: Alfred A. Knopf, 1988), 8.

3. D. H. Lawrence, *Studies in Classic American Literature* (New York: Viking Press, 1964), 51.

4. Lawrence, *Studies,* 56.

5. Leslie Fiedler, *The Return of the Vanishing American* (New York: Stein and Day, Publishers, 1968), 24.

6. Fiedler, *Vanishing American,* 164.

7. Willa Cather, *Death Comes for the Archbishop* (New York: Alfred A. Knopf, 1951), 278.

8. Cather, *Death,* 277.

9. Walt Whitman, quoted by R. W. B. Lewis, *The American Adam: Innocence, Tragedy, and Tradition in the Nineteenth Century* (Chicago and London: University of Chicago Press, 1955), 90-91.

10. Henry Nash Smith, *Virgin Land: The American West as Symbol and Myth* (Cambridge, Mass.: Harvard University Press, 1950), 82.

11. Richard Avedon, *In the American West* (New York: Harry N. Abrams, Inc., Publishers, 1985).

12. Wright Morris, *The Man Who Was There* (New York: Charles Scribner's Sons, 1945), 134-135.

13. Leo Marx, *The Machine in the Garden: Technology and the Pastoral Ideal* (New York: Oxford University Press, 1964).

14. Willa Cather, *My Antonia* (Boston and New York: Houghton Mifflin Company, 1926), 118-119.

15. Sam Peckinpah, *The Ballad of Cable Hogue,* Warner Bros., 1970.

Epilogue

1. Michael Ventura, *Shadow Dancing in the U.S.A.* (Los Angeles: Jeremy P. Taylor, Inc., 1985), 165, 173.

2. Sidra Stich, *Made in U.S.A.: An Americanization in Modern Art, the '50s and '60s* (Berkeley: University of California Press, 1987), 110.

3. Robert Adams, *Beauty in Photography: Essays in Defense of Traditional Values* (New York: Aperture, 1981), 13.

4. Harold and Peggy Samuels, eds., *The Collected Writings of Frederic Remington* (Garden City, N.J.: Doubleday, 1975), 551.

5. Peter Hassrick, *The Way West: Art of Frontier America* (New York: Harry N. Abrams, Inc., 1983), 9.

6. G. R. Swenson, "What Is Pop Art?," *Artnews,* 62 (November 1963): 26.

7. Jeffrey Rian, "An Interview with Richard Prince," *Art in America,* 75 (March 1987): 90.

8. Rian, "An Interview with Richard Prince," 90.

Index

Items in italics indicate works of art, including films and publications; boldface page numbers indicate an illustration.